CAREERS IN THE
RESTAURANT
INDUSTRY

CAREERS IN THE RESTAURANT INDUSTRY

By

Richard S. Lee

and

Mary Price Lee

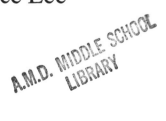
THE ROSEN PUBLISHING GROUP, Inc.

New York

Published in 1988, 1990 by The Rosen Publishing Group, Inc.
29 East 21st Street, New York, NY 10010

Revised Edition 1990

Library of Congress Cataloging-in-Publication Data

Lee, Richard S. 1927–
  Careers in the restaurant industry / by Richard S. Lee
and Mary Price Lee.
    Bibliography: p. 151
    Includes index.
    Summary: Discusses opportunities and training for jobs in the
restaurant industry, covering such aspects as fast food, franchises,
bartending, opening a restaurant, culinary education, and financial aid.
    ISBN 0-8239-1142-X
    1. Food service—Vocational guidance—Juvenile literature.
[1. Food service—Vocational guidance. 2. Vocational guidance.]
I. Lee, Mary Price. II. Title.
TX911.3.V62L44   1988
642'.5'023—dc19   87-23737

Manufactured in the United States of America

For

Randy Brown, L.P.T.
Barry Corson, M.D.
Ted Henderson, M.D.
Bruce Raffensperger, M.D.
and
Peggy Reed, R.N.
and
Susan Fuller, D.C.

Their ℞ is old-fashioned caring.

Acknowledgments

We wish to thank:
Fran Accetta, as friend, typist, and interviewee, for her good humor, patience, and interest in all our projects. We couldn't have done it without you, Fran.

And thanks for the great interviews with:
Jerry Hill, Assistant Food and Beverage Manager, Brunswick Motor Inn, Lancaster, Pennsylvania
Jerry Ortiz, Popeye's, San Juan, Puerto Rico
Gene Gosfield, co-owner of Under the Blue Moon, Chestnut Hill, Pennsylvania
Kelly Cecconi, Assistant Manager, McDonald's, Flourtown, Pennsylvania
Augustus Mandracchia, Jr., owner of Presidential Caterers, Norristown, Pennsylvania

We also appreciate the many ways people in the foodservice industry helped us. Among them are:
Richard Gaven, Senior Director, National Restaurant Association
Charles H. Sandler, Director of Educational Information, National Institute for the Foodservice Industry
Celia Niepold, Communications Specialist, National Restaurant Association
Tom Strenk, Managing Editor, *Restaurant Business Magazine*
Leslie Wolowitz, Editiorial Division, *Nation's Restaurant News*
Julie Belsterling, Director of Public Relations, and Cindy

Cummings, The Restaurant School, Philadelphia, Pennsylvania

Dr. Charles E. Clarke, Jules E. Mastbaum Area Vocational-Technical School, Philadelphia, Pennsylvania

Lena Ehrsam and Chris Garrity, Public Relations, The McDonald Corporation

William J. Burt, Director, Hotel, Restaurant and Institutional Management Program, Drexel University, Philadelphia, Pennsylvania

Finally, our appreciation to Barb Lee, who did a fine job typing parts of the manuscript.

Contents

Introducing the Number One Retail Employer in the U.S.: The Foodservice Industry

The food industry employs millions of people in its many types of service. Opportunities are greater than ever in a field that stretches from fast-food management to party catering to shipboard maitre d'.

Never has the culinary field been as exciting, challenging, and successful as it is today. A whole new spirit is at work throughout the industry.

Here are a few of the many ways foodservice is breaking new ground:

People now visit restaurants to savor the atmosphere as well as the cuisine. When they find individuality as well as quality, they spread the word. That is how many a successful restaurant is born.

Meal preparation was once strictly behind-the-scenes. Now, skillful cookery often leaves the kitchen for the television studio. Today, chefs are as common on TV talk shows as soap opera stars. And each has his or her best-selling cookbook.

Foodservice contractors now exercise greater independence as they plan meals for schools, institutions, and office building workers. They are designing "theme meals" appropriate to the region and the audience. This segment of the industry has brightened its image with such public relations tactics as having teenage star Scott Baio promote school lunch programs on television.

Another new approach: Today's restaurant manager enjoys the challenge of competition and often meets it by offering cuisine not available elsewhere.

Statistics point up the phenomenal success of the foodservice industry. The figures may appear indigestible in their size and number, but they actually go down quite nicely:

- Annual sales amount to 100 billion dollars and are growing by 10 percent each year.
- By 1995, one million more jobs will be available than there are people to fill them. In a recent year, there were 85,000 opportunities for cooks and chefs, 40,000 for dining-room attendants and dishwashers, and 70,000 for waitresses and waiters. And 20,000 more bartenders were needed to serve up refreshing drinks.

The term "foodservice" covers the entire food industry, but it may fail to convey the excitement the field now offers. It doesn't began to capture the atmosphere of an elegant buffet, the thrill of a flambéed dish, or the rambunctiousness of a McDonald's birthday party. But since the designation is comprehensive (food *and* service), it does seem to be the most appropriate term.

The National Institute for the Foodservice Industry gives this definition of foodservice: "Foodservice includes all types of establishments supplying, preparing and serving food outside the home: restaurants, carry-out operations, hotels, motels, airlines, in-plant and business operations, school and college dining rooms, hospitals, retirement centers, catering and vending companies, and food and equipment manufacturers and distributors." These many food areas represent a tremendous number of opportunities in the field.

The common denominator in foodservice work is the enjoyment of food preparation or food management. Successful foodservice employees also have a characteristic in common: They enjoy other people. "Restauranting" is not an occupation for the loner. Whether manager, waitress, salad chef, dishwasher, or food contractor, it's important to get along with other people. (This may be why the industry is often called the hospitality industry). Persons planning to open their own restaurant need an outgoing personality. They have to be accessible and affable almost around the clock.

Because most customers now approach restaurants in an upbeat way, it is not hard to be a pleasant host or hostess. As one restaurant owner says, "In the past ten years, Americans have discovered their taste buds." And, one might add, their sense of adventure. These changes in attitude nicely sum up the culinary revolution.

Chapter II

Life in the Fast-Food Lane

Fast-food restaurants are probably among your earliest memories. You grew up on the Big Mac. You argued with friends over which fast-food place had the best french fries. You made a date to meet a friend at Taco Bell.

Today, fast-food drop-ins are still popular places for young people. Hamburgers at Burger King, pizza at Pizza Hut, and roast beef at Arby's are drawing cards for the after-school munchies.

Fast-food chains reflect the wizardry of high tech. Hamburgers and stuffed baked potatoes appear, hot or packaged, almost as fast as the operator can punch the buttons that ring up the merchandise. Computers keep tabs on the deep-frying chicken and french fries.

How did these quick-serve eateries become so popular in so short a time? For one thing, they serve the on-the-run customer. Americans are always in a hurry, and now in many cases they don't even have to get out of the car to order their food. The drive-in window produces it quicker than you can say "back to work."

Another factor accounting for their popularity is that more women—single and married—are working today. This means that Mother has little time to cook dinner at the end of the day. "Let's go to Taco Bell" is the easy solution.

Mother—and Dad, too—knows that fast-food menus are fairly generous, relatively inexpensive, and of consistent quality. Food is served quickly in a clean, family-oriented atmosphere. The atmosphere has gone from the "eat-and-run" efficiency of the 1970s to today's "greenhouse" decor and a pervasive politeness that is almost amusing. Popeye's operators now ask, "Will you be dining in or out?" instead of the more familiar, "For here, or to go?"

From Arby's to Wendy's, what you eat is the product of scores of decision-makers: sales promotion and marketing specialists, executive chefs and menu planners, food procurement experts, accountants, designers, and market researchers.

Your meal is also, of course, the end product of the people in your local chain restaurant: the manager, the assistant manager, cooks, food handlers, order processors, buspeople, cashiers—and, of course, regional supervisors who keep the standards high in their assigned area.

Could you be one of these people? And which one? Should you start a fast-food career at the store level or try for a management job without behind-the-counter experience? What are the educational requirements for in-store work? For store management? What are some of the career specialties within the industry? Salary expectations? If these are some of your fast-food questions, this section has your answers—and more.

COURTESY McDONALD'S

Friendly smiles greet customers at the famous Golden Arches.

Let's start with entry-level positions where there's fast turnover. Many consider such jobs as fast-food operator or busperson as interim work. For a young person it may be fill-in time for a college break. For others, it's a way to keep busy and earn money while making final career decisions.

Grill and counter jobs at fast-food restaurants turn over on an average of six months to a year as employees return to school, advance to management, or take slower-paced jobs in other areas.

Here are some tips for getting a job at a fast-food establishment—ideas that also work well in landing any entry-level job.

When applying for a fast-food position, ask for an application at the service counter, fill out the form, and arrange for an interview with the manager. If your application is put on file because there are no openings, check with the restaurant regularly to see where you stand. Your "on hold" status may be brief because of the high turnover, so keep checking.

By the time you meet with the manager, he or she may have

COURTESY McDONALD'S

The Golden Arches offer a warm welcome across the country

checked out your references and considered your money-handling and counter experience. Managers lean toward those whose whose preferences in shifts coincide with high traffic times, so be prepared to be flexible.

Fast-food employers look for enthusiasm and interest as they interview potential employees. As one suburban fast-food manager puts it: "The person who is self-assured and pleasant during my interview is going to reflect that confidence to customers at the counter and fellow workers at the grill."

Although experience usually helps any job applicant, some fast-food managers like to hire people with no experience because then there is nothing to be unlearned. The employee who trains with a restaurant for the first time cannot practice old habits acquired in previous employment.

Before your interview, visit the restaurant and get a feel for the place. Ask employees and even customers what they know about the restaurant. What does the manager seem to look for?

COURTESY McDONALD'S

The manager offers friendly advice.

Supercleanliness? Quick action at the counter? A sunny disposition? Use the knowledge in your interview. Management will be impressed.

When it comes to money, don't hesitate to press for your fair share. Although the minimum wage is generally the starting policy, salary can sometimes be negotiable. If you have handled money as a salesperson or have worked in another fast-food restaurant, you may be able to persuade the manager that you are worth 15 cents an hour above minimum wage. If you are experienced, go ahead and ask if you can move to the next salary level before your scheduled salary-review time. (Although the salaries are low, there are compensations. Company policy encourages foodservice people to talk out problems and make suggestions about how operations can be performed better. Outside activities such as baseball games and amusement park visits are also planned to give the workers a feeling of belonging.)

Once you land the job, you have to start learning so that you can

A trainee gets some pointers from a co-worker.

keep it. First, you are given a time card, a uniform, and a training manual, and you can expect one or two days of in-training, including orientation films, possibly done in a "Simon Says" format. For instance, the film shows you how to steam Danish pastry, then *you* steam Danish pastry. The film gives instruction on pancake preparation for the breakfast menu; then you take a hand with the flapjacks at the grill.

But the real test lies not so much in the quiz at the end of the training period—standard procedure at many restaurants—as in meeting the challenges of life in the fast-food lane.

The primary endurance test for the new employee is the work pace. Be prepared to use those six hands you never knew you had. Performing your tasks "by the book" will reduce the pressure and let you get everything done. Offbeat methodology seldom works out.

You can also make things easier by not throwing up your own roadblocks. For instance, if you have signed on for certain hours,

Staff members check the records.

stick to them. Hours are a particularly sensitive point with managers, and you are asking for trouble if you change signals. The same goes for bringing personal irritations to work. They do not belong in a job that depends as much on attitude as on skill.

Succeeding in fast-food work is not so very different from meeting the challenge of most minimum-training jobs. There are certain constants: a positive initial interview, an opportunity to negotiate hours and pay, a specified training period, and perseverance in a fast-paced job.

Entry-level positions have going for them something that some executive and professional jobs cannot claim: consistency. The fortunes of a chemical engineer, for instance, may rise and fall as consumer demand affects company policy. An auto salesperson may have a job today but not tomorrow. But there is always work in areas that cater to people's daily needs. With a positive attitude and willingness to work, you can make the rapid turnover of such

COURTESY McDONALDS'S

Drive-through windows speed the hungry traveler.

positions a turning point for you. You can find life in the fast-food lane very rewarding.

Jerry Ortiz is a fast-food operator. Operators are not *waiters* or *waitresses* because they don't generally leave the service counter. Jerry works at San Juan Popeye's. That's right, San Juan, Puerto Rico. Fast-food restaurants are plentiful on this beautiful island, and they also dot the globe from Japan to Venezuela. As a fast-food operator, Jerry has to meet the same standards of service as his counterparts in the States. People from Popeye's headquarters in New Orleans check in frequently to see that Jerry's work and the operation of the restaurant service measure up.

Noon to 1:30 P.M. is the San Juan Popeye's "busy time," just as it is everywhere else. But with tourists to serve as well as the island population, the workers at Popeye's may need even more spinach to keep up with the crowds.

Popeye's, Wendy's, McDonald's and other fast-food restaurants provide tours on request. Kelly Cecconi, First Assistant Manager of the McDonald's Restaurant in Flourtown, Pennsylvania, recently gave an interested customer a glimpse of their multifaceted activities and streamlined equipment. The visitor was shown how McDonald's cooks its french fries to just the right texture and taste. She saw how computers are used to regulate the cooking of the hamburgers. She watched a demonstration of the ice cream machine, where cool and creamy swirls fall into a waiting cup.

Not all of the action takes place on the customer floor. Downstairs in the stockroom is a walk-in refrigerator where tomatoes and lettuce are stored for the McD.L.T.s. Soft drinks for the service counter are actually mixed from syrup and carbonated water in the stockroom and pumped to the dispensers above.

Kelly originally held an entry-level position. Her cheeriness and industry led to a promotion. Like Kelly, many beginners are interested in fast-food jobs with greater responsibility. With training, they can become assistant manager, then manager, and finally perhaps supervisor of a number of stores.

Dunkin' Donuts, for instance, has a "Step-Up-to-Excellence" program that encourages workers to rise to managerial ranks. Wendy's, Burger King, and Taco Bell, among others, have extensive management training programs. Wendy's, with over

2,500 stores across the country, prepares assistant managers by immersing them in a four- to seven-week program during which they study the company manuals, work in the restaurant under supervision, and attend classroom sessions. Trainees learn everything from counter management to food ordering.

The McDonald's qualifications for manager generally apply to all fast-food companies. They include some experience in the fast-food business, a sincere desire to make a career in restaurant management, and a college degree, if possible. (The right attitude and *aptitude* may substitute for the degree.)

Salaries for assistant managers range from $12,740 to $16,700, co-managers $14,300 to $18,377, and store managers $18,200 to $25,000. Benefits include vacations and medical and life insurance. (Salaries and benefits vary according to restaurant and restaurant chain. Salaries may match or exceed those mentioned, and benefit packages may include such extras as scholarship programs.)

A manager sets the tone of a place, so it's important that he or she be an effective leader. Fast-food restaurants have their share of poor managers who often make enemies among the service workers by being abusive and impatient. But then, a manager's patience is often tried. He or she may end up doing the service worker's jobs (if the staff is short) as well as his own. Unless you are easygoing yet energetic and industrious, don't try for a fast-food managership. You'll find that your fries will burn up and *you* will burn *out*.

Managerial duties of fast-food restaurants overlap. For instance, most managers learn how to cook the food so they can judge the quality of the products in their kitchen. Dunkin' Donuts managers enjoy this aspect of the training because the product they sell is a universal favorite. Imagine learning how to make over twenty varieties of doughnuts and tasting the results!

Burger King, the second-largest hamburger fast-food chain in America, employs over 20,000 workers. Their ten training centers give the prospective manager an intensive five-week course that includes health inspection, public relations, and even psychology. (What if someone comes up and says "Where's the beef?"!) The instructional period combines classroom work and on-the-job training.

Taco Bell has a different approach, and that's what Glen Bell wanted back in 1962. Bell felt there was a fast-food market for something more unusual than hamburgers and fried chicken. Fifteen hundred Taco Bell restaurants later, it appears he was right. The company's profits are increasing 20 percent annually, proving that south-of-the-border food can be popular north-of-the-border, too.

If you are interested in becoming a manager in a Taco Bell restaurant, you will put in a five-week stint of basic training, both in-house and in the classroom. You'll learn about operational procedures, store marketing, and equipment. If all goes well and you move from assistant manager to full manager, your future may include multimanagement: supervising up to eight restaurants.

Several years ago, a newspaper decided to run a contest to see which fast-food restaurant made the best hamburger. The taste-testers were not adults, but kids. Blindfolded, they judged the comparative merits of Burger King's Whopper, McDonald's Big Mac, and the Wendy hamburger. Results were mixed. Said one youngster, "I give the Big Mac an 11, on a scale of 1 to 10." Another said, "Wendy's is OK, but, yuck, the lettuce!"

Another light note to a serious business: Robots were installed to operate as foodservice workers in a Canadian fast-food restaurant. They performed competently until misprogramming caused chaos in the restaurant. The dutiful mechanoids dumped the french fries into the milkshakes, as ordered. What a delicious dish to set before—the public!

Ghaleb Mikki, manager of the Harvard Street McDonald's in Brookline, Massachusetts, is as interested as anyone else in the quality of the food he sells. But once a year, he features a different form of refreshment when his employees hand out *water* to the Boston Marathoners as they stream past his restaurant. A nice touch, and a good way to get some free advertising.

Mikki and managers in other fast-food chains are aware that not all of their customers are just dropping in for a Big Mac. Some have been sent by the parent company to snoop. Hired "mystery shoppers" pose as customers to evaluate a store for service, quality, and cleanliness. They then turn in monthly reports that determine a store's ratings. These sleuths order a meal and dash back to their car to stick a thermometer into the food to see how hot it is. Store personnel never know who these visitors are; they just hope the mystery guests receive good service and food.

For further information concerning managership, here are several contacts in the large field of fast foods:

Personnel Director
Wendy's International
4208 West Dublin Granville Road
P.O. Box 256
Dublin, OH 43017

Personnel Director
Burger King Corporation
P.O. Box 5Q0783, Biscayne Annex
Miami, FL 33152

Director of Human Resources
Taco Bell
P.O. Box C19596,
Irvine, CA 92713

Director of Personnel
McDonald's Corporation
McDonald's Plaza
Oak Brook, IL 60521

Keep an eye out, too, in the "help wanted" section of your newspaper.

* * *

Of course you can be in the fast-food business and never deep-fry a Chicken McNugget. At the national headquarters of the various fast-food restaurants, the accent is on sizzling ideas, not sizzling french fries. Competition is fierce to stay on top or leapfrog to the top.

Although some fast-food empires have outside agencies do their national and regional advertising and public relations, others have in-house departments. If you like to write about food and have had writing experience, you might enjoy dealing with it from the public relations angle. And there would be plenty to write about. No restaurant group highlights its food as energetically as the fast-food kings.

For instance if one chain comes out with a new food gimmick that lures customers to its counters, rival corporations scurry to capture the lost market with their own revolutionary ideas. These struggles are headlined in the business sections of newspapers: "Hot Potato Is Main Course in Latest Fast Food Battle"; "Burger Wars Move to New Battlegrounds"; "Pizza Hut Wants a Bigger Slice," etc.

You may feel that food advertising is not really a food-oriented career. Nonetheless, as a wordsmith, you would be dealing with food or food-related topics all day. And your best ideas have to be mouth-watering to be successful.

Fast-food companies gain ground on other chains by establishing stores in unexpected locales: at zoos, at miltary bases, even in hospitals. Because of the number and diversity of locations and the availability of jobs through high turnover, these new locations open up job possibilities for *everyone*. For people and groups who find work hard to find, the many openings—including managership placement—are welcome opportunities.

These many job openings produce some exciting statistics. The National Institute for the Foodservice Industry reports more than 30,000 openings annually in fast foods. The Vocational Clubs of America *Journal* predicts that the 1990s will see 297,000 job openings in food preparation, with the bulk of them in counter-service types of restaurants. When you consider that 40 percent of the money we spend when eating out is spent at fast-food chains, the great number of job openings is not surprising.

Efforts to move or stay ahead filter right down to extracurricular activities in the individual stores. Managers receive calendars with promotion ideas appropriate to the month or season. McDonald's, for instance, highlights February as Black History Month. Local schools are offered kits and films that make Black history more vivid.

No one would want to place a bet on who will stay on top or lose market share in the fast-foods game. As long as creative minds battle for the public's attention and dollars, forecasting the outcome is as tough as predicting a lottery winner.

A final word on the whole *very big* subject of fast food: It has provided countless jobs for the young and the not-so-young for several decades. It will continue to be one of the best sources of employment and advancement. Working in fast foods also offers a solid base of experience for any restaurant or foodservice business you may choose to enter.

Chapter III

Owning and Operating a Franchised Restaurant

To many restaurateurs, owning a franchise—or more than one—is the ultimate achievement. Certainly, franchises are profitable, especially those with proven success and high-traffic locations.

Most restaurant franchises are fast-food outlets such as McDonald's, Kentucky Fried Chicken, Taco Bell, and a baker's dozen more. The food may differ, but the format is much the same: Customers carry their own food from the order counter to tables or booths, or claim their order at a drive-through window. Other franchises are "family restaurants" with table service, a wider food selection at still-moderate prices, and usually no drive-up or take-out service.

In any case, a franchisee owns and operates his or her own chain restaurant under a license granted by the parent corporation. Most franchising corporations also operate "company stores," staffed by salaried managers, but each outlet of a given franchise has its own "trade area." All restaurant supplies and many if not all foods and ingredients are bought from the parent corporation, its subsidiaries, or authorized distributors. In a successful operation, food prices should assure profit for both the corporation and the franchisee.

Competition among fast-food franchises is often wild and woolly, since many franchisees select the same geographic area, based on their individual evaluations of a particular market.

Training is taken seriously by corporations and franchisees alike. It takes up to two years for a first-time McDonald's franchisee to complete training at the corporation's Hamburger

University and nearby McDonald's outlets. And once the franchised restaurant has opened, it must be operated strictly by the corporate book (a gigantic manual in the case of McDonald's). The corporation establishes the expected—and high—standards of quality, service, cleanliness, and value. Corporation inspectors—often posing as customers—visit franchised outlets frequently to double-check performance. While the franchisees run all the risks associated with the restaurant business, they get plenty of help from headquarters.

This guidance is a major asset, especially to people coming into fast-food and family restaurant operation without earlier food-service experience, as some do. Another franchise benefit is the strong name recognition and public acceptance generated by national and regional advertising. Although much of the cost is paid by the franchisees, they are the ones who benefit from the customers lured by special prices, premiums, or just good-looking food shown in TV commercials.

Franchises aren't for everyone, however. A creative chef or innovative restaurateur would feel stifled by corporate regulations and inflexible recipes. And while long hours are common in the restaurant business, 65- to 80-hour weeks are not unusual in franchise operation, especially for the boss. In addition to long daily hours—often from 6:00 A.M. to 11:00 P.M. and sometimes 24 hours a day—time is also needed for all the normal restaurant paperwork, plus the reports that must be filed with the parent company.

A would-be franchisee may also have to relocate to obtain a desirable franchise in a part of the country where the chain is still expanding and competition is less severe.

Another drawback is money—or the lack of it. Franchisees must pay fees ranging from $6,500 to $45,000 for the right to use such symbols as the big Western hat, the mission bell, or the golden arches, But that's only the beginning. From $76,000 to $650,000 *more* must be available to build and equip the new outlet. When a franchisee's business reputation or personal credit is good, banks may lend much of this money. In certain cases, the franchising corporation will lease the restaurant to the franchisee for several years, until it is operating successfully. Then the franchisee can borrow the money to buy it, based on the restaurant's performance, and repay the loan from future profits.

Profitable it can be, too. The average McDonald's brings in $1.26 *million* its first year, before expenses and taxes. Taco Bell, a fast-growing chain with a Mexican food theme, has average yearly sales of $575,000 to $600,000 per outlet. Taco Bell is considered a better return on investment by some because its franchise fee and capital investment run $190,000 to $253,000 compared to the $298,000 to $352,000 needed for a McDonald's franchise. Also, a Taco Bell can be operating in 60 to 90 days; the wait for a McDonald's is 18 months or longer.

For those whose pocketbooks are a bit less fat, other specialty food outlets can be franchised for less. The Domino's Pizza chain, for instance, had a 1984 franchise fee of $6,500 and a minimum capital requirement of $76,000. A baskin-Robbins ice cream store can be franchised for $25,000 to $50,000. A franchise for a Cookies Factory comes to $80,000.

Chapter IV

Maitre d', Bartender, Waiter/ Waitress: The People Who Meet the Public

The maitre d'*, host, or hostess is the first person to greet the incoming restaurant customer. He or she is in full charge of the dining room. A warm, welcoming smile and smooth, efficient seating can be the prelude to a pleasant meal.

The work is low-key—until a place gets busy!—as the hostess or host greets guests and escorts them to freshly set tables. Table seating can be tricky because the host/hostess must often save large tables for groups with reservations, juggle seating times, assign "stations" (groups of tables) to waiters and waitresses, and generally manage a dining room much like a very big, and very busy, game board.

The host/hostess may also have other duties, such as cashier, waitress/waiter supervisor, and general director. Just as does the restaurant manager—and at times, even more so—this individual helps set the tone of the establishment, the "feeling" that customers receive about it.

In many restaurants, young people have worked their way up from busboy/girl to maitre d'. Keith Gessler, maitre d' of the elegant Flanders Hotel in Ocean City, New Jersey, was one who took his career right to the top.

In the summers of his college years, he bused at The Flanders,

---

* Maître d'hôtel, "master of the hostelry" in literal English, is the correct French term, but it is little used. The presence of a maitre d' usually distinguishes a fancy restaurant from a simpler one.

gradually taking on greater responsibility in the dining rooms. After college, Keith attended the Academy of Culinary Arts of Atlantic Community College, graduating with an Associate of Applied Science degree in hospitality management.

The knowledge gained there and at the hotel led to Keith's appointment as maitre d'. This young man's meteoric rise is a classic example of the opportunity to grow within the field.

The waiter/waitress is the person the public knows best. He or she interacts with the customer from the time beverages are ordered and menus are presented, to settling the check. Waiter or waitress duties appear obvious. They include taking an order, serving each course of the meal in an appetizing way, tallying up the check, and accepting cash or a credit card as payment. But, straightforward as these duties may sound, it is the way they are performed that can make or mar a dining experience.

The average customer is often not aware that the waitress or waiter is at work long before the restaurant is open to the public. Waiters/waitresses set the tables with proper utensils and glassware. They often have to memorize a list of "specials" and explain the unique ingredients or the cooking process of each. This information may be supplied by the kitchen just before the first guests step in the door.

Clearing a table is an art. The waiter/waitress must remove dishes constantly as the meal progresses, yet give the customers the feeling that they may take their time. Once the dining room is closed, waiters/waitresses change tablecloths or place mats and either reset the tables or leave them ready for resetting for the next day or the next meal.

This job really demands an outgoing, energetic person, one who is sympathetic yet professional about every step that must be done time after time, table after table.

Howard Fineman of Levittown, Pennsylvania, broke into a most unusual waitering job. Howard worked in the dining room of a casino in Atlantic City, New Jersey, where he had to serve up solace as well as filet of sole. Many big bettors came from gaming tables to dining table, short on money and manners (some who had lost heavily expected free meals!). Howard, handsome and friendly, gave them careful attention and an opportunity to relax over a well-served dinner.

Most waiters/waitresses, like Howard, get their experience on the job (in his case, work at a country club was his entrée to the casino job). There are few schools that teach one how to be a good waiter/waitress, but if you have an opportunity, take food service courses in high school. Some waiting skills are usually included.

In the mid-1980s, waiters/waitresses were paid an average of $2.04 to $3.64 an hour, excluding tips. Salaries are small because tips are expected to bring in a sizable amount of money. Of course, salary and tips both depend on the particular restaurant; work in a family restaurant will net a modest income per meal (and modest tips as well), but customer turnover is fast. The waiter/waitress in a top-quality restaurant may make up to $22,000 a year.

Someone who knows the quality restaurant field from firsthand experience is Francesca MacAron. She works in a famous restaurant, perhaps the finest in New York—The Four Seasons. Mac-Aron finds pluses and minuses in a job that includes serving world-famous celebrities. In her first days on the job, she was exhausted, weepy, and extra-sensitive to criticism. The hours were also upsetting: an 11:00 A.M. to 3:00 P.M. shift one day, a 5:00 P.M. to 1:00 A.M. stint the next.

But as Francesca became used to such things as being responsible for the elaborate table settings—three spoons of various sizes, plus knives, on the right, forks in ascending order on the left—she began to feel at home in the job. Being comfortable was a matter of learning to pace herself.

The job is also bringing in money for what Francesca *really* wants to do: sing full-time with a band she has organized. In the meantime, she says, "Being a waitress has made me learn about the real world and what it takes to make a living."

Although many people enjoy waiting on tables, a common complaint is that a restaurant "overbooks" the serving people. Waiters and waitresses find themselves responsible for more tables than they can comfortably handle. If a waiter proves he can handle four tables, he will be given five. If a waitress courteously and capably covers five tables, the restaurant assigns six.

Restaurants like these do not care about the comfort of their customers—*or* their waiters. They simply want to get top dollar from their employees, even at the expense of good customer service. This can lead to burnout for waiters and waitresses and a bad reputation for the restaurant.

Knowing that this situation exists, try to assess a restaurant's attitude toward its employees. Drop in at mealtime and see if the waiters look frazzled and rushed. If they appear, on the other hand, to be serving at an efficient, realistic pace, then you can expect to be doing the same.

Jobs as waiter or waitress are available now, and the future seems equally promising. The Vocational Industrial Clubs of America *Journal* foresees 562,000 new jobs up to and into the 1990s for waiters and waitresses. In fact, the need for these service people will double in the next ten years or so.

Another visible worker on the restaurant scene is the bartender. And incidentally, the bartender is no longer automatically male. Women have been tending bar for quite some time now and are proving to be capable mixologists—a fancy title for a bartender's work.

Using the word loosely, mixology could well apply to the bartender's ability as a "mixer," because he or she must enjoy meeting people. Since bartenders are generally confined to a space the size of a dog kennel run for 8 to 10 hours a day, they count on their customers to bring variety, entertainment—and, sometimes, problems—to their work.

A good bartender must be able to make a variety of drinks at assembly-line speed. Bartenders must also maintain stock, keep inventory records, and be responsible for "spillage" (only a certain amount of wastage is tolerated). Like other food service people, bartenders and barmaids must appear relaxed while thirsty crowds await their creations.

In most restaurants with bar service, wine selection and inventory are among the bartender's responsibilities. In finer restaurants that emphasize the quality and variety of their wines, a wine steward or sommelier is in charge. He or she is responsible for developing and maintaining a cellar combining wines of good value and exceptionally rare, costly vintages. The specialized knowledge needed for such a post is rarely self-taught but usually acquired in a training program in culinary school or in college-level courses in restaurant management/dining room operation.

Anyone dispensing alcoholic beverages must be at least of legal drinking age in the area of work; most must be 21. In many cases, a man or woman 25 years old or older is preferred. There are bartending schools, but, like waiting table, most drink-mixing skills are learned on the job as assistant to an experienced bartender. Positions in this field are available year-round, but resort areas in season offer particularly good opportunities. Again like waiting tables, the Vocational Industrial Clubs of America *Journal* reports a bright bartending future: 121,000 new jobs in the 1990s.

Chapter **V**

Managing a Restaurant: Wearing All Hats Including the Chef's

Most restaurant managers would like to have an extra pair of eyes, an extra pair of hands, and feet that never get tired. That's because this employee often has to be in two places at one time. Included in the duties are such details as seeing that waitresses' caps are straight and being sure the food is of consistently high quality.

Restaurant management is exciting and demanding. Jerry Hill proves this as he pursues his career as Assistant Food and Beverage Manager of the Brunswick Motor Inn, in downtown Lancaster, Pennsylvania.

The Brunswick is tastefully modern and efficient. The hotel's focal point is the tourist trade, and for the tourists the center of attention is a group known as the Amish, the Plain People, or the Pennsylvania Dutch.

Many bus tour operators use the Brunswick as their stopover when they bring groups to the Amish country. Mostly family farmers and Old World craftspeople, the Amish avoid such worldly things as automobiles and electricity. At the end of a day of viewing farms and passing buggies, the tour-bus visitors are eager for an ample down-home meal.

The Brunswick plans its food and service around its guests' straightforward tastes. "We stay away from flambées and other frills," explains Jerry Hill. "Our people aren't looking for them, and those touches can add considerably to your costs." Food cost is only one of Jerry's concerns; he wears numerous other hats in his job.

29

On a typical evening in the tourist season (from mid-April to mid-November), Jerry may be responsible for three scheduled banquets plus the smooth operation of the hotel's two restaurants, the Copper Kettle and Bernhardt's. Commenting on the evening, he says, "We may be serving the Paragon tour people their roast beef dinner in one room while taking care of the Tauck Tour crowd in another banquet room."

The Brunswick also attracts companies conducting middle-management conferences and visitors doing business in this friendly Pennsylvania town. Amtrak, for instance, booked nine thousand hotel rooms in a recent year to house middle-management railroad people for training programs. This business is a windfall for the hotel. For Jerry Hill, it translates into a busy career.

Jerry may do a little bit of everything as part of the Brunswick management team, but specifically, his end of the business is *service*. Service concerns people—waiters, waitresses, bartenders, and customers. At banquets, he confers with a corporate conference manager or a bus tour director. They coordinate all the details of a well-run dinner, checking the number of people expected, perhaps arranging for a projector and screen, and deciding on what time the meal may be expected to end so that the banquet room can be prepared for the next event.

Often, Jerry's banquet role is amiable disciplinarian. "People have so much fun at get-togethers preceding the banquet that we have a hard time getting them to come to dinner. When you realize that a meal is set for a specific time, and that you must serve soup and salad before the main course, it gets pretty hairy when people don't take their places. Food can't be left standing on steam tables for too long. So, I have to find the person in charge to round up the flock."

Jerry Hill is involved with anything and everything to do with food or beverages. On a given day, he may stock a bar, help plan menus, conduct a food inventory, check the condition of the incoming produce and meat, and supervise a banquet.

In season, Jerry averages sixty hours a week. When asked how he survives such a schedule, he replies, "I don't take my work home with me." At home, Jerry's mind is off the food course and on the golf course. And that's the way it should be.

Jerry would be well qualified for the unfilled position described in a recent want-ad:

ASSISTANT
DIRECTOR OF
FOOD AND BEVERAGE

We have an excellent opportunity for a
management professional experienced in
front and back-of-the-house operating
services to assist in directing and
overseeing the food and beverage department
operations. The successful candidate we
seek will have a minimum of 3 years' com-
parable experience, preferably in a similar
size facility. We offer an excellent salary
and benefits package along with a solid
career path. For consideration, apply in
person or forward résumé to:

Jerry's duties are fairly specific. What are the duties of a restaurant manager? Restaurant managers are responsible for the work of all employees under them, and they oversee the purchasing of food and equipment. They must also know all the prevailing health and sanitation regulations and see that they are observed.

Added to this list of responsibilities are the clerical and financial duties. Detailed records must be kept; payroll requires careful bookkeeping. And on top of all that, the manager must create an atmosphere that inspires confidence in his customers. As a person of many responsibilities, the manager must appear to have none!

Restaurant managers need stamina. The job requires walking miles and miles without ever leaving the restaurant or hotel. It's also helpful to have a sympathetic nature. Plenty can go wrong—in the kitchen, in the dining rooms, in banquet planning. The manager is the "emergency brake"; his or her swift actions usually keep problems to a minimum.

How do you gain enough experience to become a restaurant manager? You have several ways to go about it. Climb the ladder by starting at an entry-level position and work your way up. Waiting on tables, for instance, may lead to pantry supervisor and on up.

A surer way to gain access to management jobs is to take courses in foodservice management and restaurant administration. Two-year associate degree programs at a community college or four-year programs leading to a degree will prepare you for immediate entry into restaurant management. (See Chapter XI on education in this field.)

A question of universal interest: How much can you earn as a restaurant manager? The answer depends largely on your experience and the size, location, and type of restaurant. As a result, there is no *typical* salary in this field. If you're a college graduate with a degree in some phase of restaurant work, you can expect to earn $13,600 to $14,800. (This salary generally includes a good benefits package.) Noncollege trainees generally start at a lower salary level. For the experienced manager of an up-scale restaurant, salary can range from $25,000 to $40,000 yearly.

Opportunities in restaurant management are excellent, particularly for those with academic qualifications. The fact that one in every seven foodservice people is a restaurant manager indicates that chances are good for this top-level job. *Working Woman* magazine, in its issue of July 1986, cites restaurant manager as one of the top 25 careers for women in the United States.

Restaurant managers are in demand because there are so many places where they can practice their skills. Hotels, motels, clubs, resorts, steamships, factories, and schools all need restaurant supervisors.

"Chain" restaurants also are often on the lookout for capable managers. Denny's, a large national chain, is a good example. These dependable restaurants are open 24 hours daily and are known for good, family-oriented food in pleasant, all-American surroundings.

Denny's needs large numbers of managers and "unit" managers to oversee employees numbering in the thousands. (The Denny's chain has some 50,000 employees, including managers.) Future managers are trained to be leaders and go through an extensive orientation program. When they have completed the course, they are ready to represent Denny's.

The future Denny's manager must have a liberal arts degree or culinary experience. And something encouraging for Denny's entry-level people: All vacancies are filled from within if candidates meet the above qualifications.

The salary and benefit program is excellent, with "perks" such as dental insurance and profit sharing.

* * *

Another important area related to restaurant management is foodservice *contractors* who operate cafeterias and concessions in industrial plants, colleges, and corporations.

People trained in this area may have as many as ten "accounts" or agreements with organizations to supply their food needs. Thus the annual sales for a person handling ten accounts can amount to as much as ten million dollars.

The typical foodservice contractor intern spends about six months in intensive on-the-job training. Trainees learn all the kitchen functions as well as managerial responsibilities such as inventory and ordering and receiving food. As an initial assignment, they may find themselves responsible for a company that serves 600 meals a day. As trainees move into managership programs, their companies may assign them to institutions involving 1,200 meals a day.

Among the largest foodservice contractors are Saga, Macke, and ARA Services. Jeanne Clark, an ARA employee, is Assistant Food Service Manager for Widener University's campus in Chester, Pennsylvania. Jeanne enjoys the challenge of keeping faculty and students pleased with their meals three times a day, seven days a week. Five managers report to her daily as she supervises the unit's 80 employees. This all adds up to a strenuous but exciting job.

Part of the fun of a campus contract is the freedom to design meals that are imaginative. Jeanne supervises make-your-own-crêpe nights, "Ice Cream Sundae" bars, and top-your-hot-dog stands. Football games give her the opportunity to plan tempting cookouts near the playing field.

Speaking of football, the Philadelphia Eagles' summer training camp is a fixture of suburban West Chester University of Pennsylvania. Here, Service America, a dining services company, feeds

125 ravenously hungry football players every meal, every day.

Frank Bell, the coordinator between the Eagles' training staff and Service America, addresses the issue of serving three bountiful yet healthful meals. The meals—strong on fruits and vegetables—are prepared in volume, but Bell tries nonetheless to give them a home-made flavor.

What's the most popular item on the players' menu? In Philadelphia's hot, steamy summer weather, it's ice cream, of course. In fact, before the football players turn in for the night, they polish off a "snack"—15 gallons of ice cream.'

Service America meets the high standards that foodservice contracting demands. But the contractors and their employees have ample opportunity to add their own touches to whatever they do. Even when it involves serving enough ice cream to make an igloo!

Chapter VI

Cook and Chef: The Cornerstones of a Good Restaurant

It's no news that cooks and chefs establish a restaurant's reputation with their fine cuisine. What *is* news is that a few can claim a chef's hat before they are out of their teens! For those of you who are still in high school, here are profiles of three ambitious, talented young people who are already established cooks.

John Righi of Philadelphia can prepare a hundred dinners a night—a tall order for a sixteen-year-old. But John has hung around a kitchen for as long as he can remember. That's because his parents operate a restaurant where he learned to roll a piecrust at about the same time he conquered his ABCs.

John's first official job was busboy at Mama Yolanda's Restaurant, the family business named after his grandmother. He admired the activity and concentration of the cooks as he made his repeated runs into the kitchen. Often, when all his tables were cleared and the chef had left for the night, John would try out a few of the evening's specials himself.

The young entrepreneur became so good that he was often called into service as a sort of "side man." John would help the master chef by making the pastas and watching dishes as they browned under the broiler.

Within months, John was hired by the chef of a nearby Italian restaurant to make the staples of Italian cuisine: tortellinis, cannellonis, and fettucine. Now he is back in the family restaurant—with a staff of three who work for him, a major feat for such a young chef.

Miles away in Minersville, Pennsylvania, another sixteen-year-old, Jeff Cleary, spends twelve or more hours a day making bread and pastries for his own bakery. It all started when Jeff's sister was trying to win the Homecoming Queen crown in her high school. To raise money for her campaign against the other nominees, Jeff baked countless loaves of bread and cinnamon buns.

Jeff's vo-tech food preparation program accounts for much of his success as a baker. But his instructor also credits Jeff's mouth-watering creations to his natural talents in the kitchen.

Jeff's future plans include a culinary college where he can learn the whole range of cooking skills. In the meantime, he continues to fill his small store with the aroma of baking bread.

Another young chef may soon join Jeff Cleary and John Righi as a junior star of the kitchen. The Philadelphia School District sponsors an annual competition for student Chef of the Year. A recent year's cook-off was won by Nicola Shirley, a senior at the city's Germantown High School.

To win the title, Nicola matched cooking skills against students from other Philadelphia public schools. She easily outdistanced them with a born-to-cook performance: poached salmon with ginger-lime butter sauce. Experienced chefs judged all contestants' performances on the basis of work plan, techniques, and appearance and taste of the finished product.

Nicola has long had her eye on a career as a chef. Winning the competition not only gave her awards, but added to her experience. Besides a certificate of commendation and a $50 U.S. Savings Bond, she won a week's apprenticeship at La Famiglia, one of Philadelphia's premier restaurants.

Some may feel that "winning" a week of hard work is not exactly a special gift! But for Nicola it meant working with people among the best in the field.

La Famiglia was so impressed with Nicola's apprentice work that they asked her back for management training when she finished school. The young champion was delighted. "I've always wanted to be a chef," she said. "It's going to take hard work and long hours, but with determination, I know my dream will come true. I know I will be successful." With that attitude and her already extensive experience, there's no doubt that Nicola will be one of tomorrow's top chefs.

Most chefs are much older than John, Jeff, or Nicola. In fact, many have put in years of apprenticeship before they could officially wear a chef's hat. The white "puffed soufflé" hat may be worn by a chef or a cook, but the two positions are not interchangeable. While chefs may be cooks, cooks are not necessarily chefs. Cooks generally have less formal training and do not have the encompassing responsibilities of the chef. Cooks can plan menus, prepare various dishes, and taste-test the food being prepared. The chef's primary responsibility in a large establishment is to supervise the activities of the cooks who specialize in certain dishes. Chefs also develop recipes that will enhance their reputation. In the smaller restaurant—especially when the chef is also the owner—the chef may do all the cooking, with little if any extra help.

In the following pages, "chef" and "cook" may be used interchangeably, with the understanding that there are differences between the two.

Short-order or diner-restaurant cooks generally offer food "standards"—wholesome but usually predictable dishes. They also do not have the responsibilities of cooks and chefs in larger or more elaborate restaurants.

Chefs or cooks in charge of restaurants are responsible for the quality and preparation of all the foods they serve. This balancing act combines culinary talent with timing, good judgment, and supervisory skills.

As director of a large kitchen, a chef may supervise a sous-chef (or under-chef), soup chef, sauce chef, vegetable chef, and pastry chef. The chef may have trained these assistants over a period of time, beginning with basic lessons in chopping and blending and gradually moving on to more complex dishes. Or it may be his or her job to recruit assistant chefs from culinary schools or other restaurants and blend them successfully into the "mix" of his or her kitchen. The chef must also confer with stewards, the general manager, and catering/banquet managers.

While chefs' work may be stimulating and the task of overseeing the output of under-chefs a challenge, the bottom line is that they must turn a profit. That is why major hotels and resorts have executive chefs. This career requires a good head for organizing, food planning, menu pricing, and accurately determining the cost of needed equipment and staff. Every chef needs a good degree of executive ability to make these decisions, even if on a smaller scale.

Here is a typical day's duty list for a master chef or head cook:

Duty 1: Plan the menu of the day. This may have been done ahead, and the ingredients purchased so that they are on hand for preparation.

Duty 2: Examine the ingredients in a final check of quality, freshness, and appearance. Knowledgeable chefs can be absolute tyrants at inspection time.

Duty 3: Prepare the recipes. Large portions of ingredients are measured, prepared, and mixed. Soups, sauces, casseroles, fish, and meats are made ready for baking or broiling, mixing or heating. The chef is everywhere, sniffing, tasting—determined that all dishes leaving the kitchen will please the customers.

Duty 4: Fill diners' orders. Meats are sliced and served on plates with vegetables arranged attractively and garnishes in place. Only then are platters ready to leave the kitchen.

Duty 5: Maintain standards. Chefs and cooks in medium-size and large restaurants are generally not involved in washing up. However, they have an overall responsibility to see that the kitchen is in good order, up to standards for the next day's, or the next shift's, meals.

Chefs and cooks work with their assistants as a team. They produce under pressure, usually in close quarters, with smoke, confusion, and clatter as their companions. It helps if the chef is unflappable. The kitchen staff appreciates a cool head, too.

Training for chef or head cook can take a variety of routes (see also Chapter XI on food service education). Here are a few ways to work your way to this key position in a restaurant, hotel, resort, or cruise ship.

A vocational or trade high school offering chef's training may be available. Many community colleges and four-year institutions offer similar instruction on a more sophisticated level. The American Culinary Federation offers apprenticeship and certification pro-

COOK AND CHEF   **39**

grams; for information write to P.O. Box 30466, St. Augustine, FL 32084.

As we have seen, a chef is a cook, planner, and business person all at once. So whether you start training in high school or college, it's a good idea to take business mathematics and business administration courses; they can be invaluable in managing a successful kitchen.

School service divisions of state departments of education cooperate with many vo-tech schools. They often offer help to the school-educated cafeteria worker who wants to become a chef.

Chef training is also available if you join the armed forces. Quality chef/cook training programs can help young people find a job fairly quickly after finishing military duty.

Most new chefs serve an apprenticeship for several years after graduating from a culinary school or gaining some culinary experience. This apprenticeship gives them a working relationship with a master chef and opportunity to become qualified by the American Culinary Federation.

An alternative to formal chef training is simply to start at the beginning and work your way up. (A high school diploma is advisable no matter what route you take.) But if you are planning ahead to reach the top, be sure that your employer knows your mind and that your job offers advancement possibilities.

Jobs may be found through employment bureaus, trade associations and unions, and state employment agencies. Or take a look at the newspaper want-ads. You may find employment opportunities like these:

HEAD COOK

Your cooking skills will be
appreciated at a camp
in the Pocono Mountains of
Pennsylvania. At least two
years' related exp. required
to work as part of a team
to coordinate and prepare all
meals. Must be familiar with

operating electric and steam
cooking equipment. Salary
for season, $3,500. Send
résumé to...

CHEF

200-seat suburban restau-
rant seeks achievement-
oriented professional with
mgt. background. Exp. in
N. Italian and current
California cuisine desired.
$26,000 + medical benefits.
Send résumé to...

CHEF

Sat. Lunch/Sun. Brunch, full
chg. of fast-paced, ultra-
modern kitchen. B182, News.

Chefs and cooks, like others in the foodservice industry, appear to have ample opportunity for work. The Vocational Industrial Clubs of America *Journal* expects 402,000 new jobs for chefs and cooks in the 1990s. These jobs are found in private clubs, on steamships, in institutions and government installations, and in airline catering services as well as restaurants.

Also, people today have more leisure time to spend on vacations and all-day excursions. These trips almost always include meals out, usually in resort and tourist restaurants.

Just as food services vary widely, so do hours. They vary according to the restaurant or institution, but it is safe to say that they seldom follow the typical workday. A restaurant may be open to customers from 11:30 A.M. to 9:00 P.M., but the attending chef is working long before the doors open and often far past closing time (generally, a long shift such as this is shared). Holidays, weekends, special scheduled parties, and even unexpected crowds may also lead to overtime.

What wages can be expected in exchange for long hours? They vary according to the size, type, and location of employment. If you really want to earn dollars, go *West*, young man—or woman. According to a recent survey, the large, well-known Western hotels pay chefs and cooks the country's highest average wages.

In general, the median salary for chefs is $23,000 and for executive chefs, $30,500. Cooks of various kinds earn $5 to $8.50 an hour, and assistants' earnings range from $3.75 to $6 an hour.

"Chef," until fairly recently, meant *male*. No longer. Women—who have always cooked in the home kitchen—now cook for the public. They are gaining recognition as chefs in top-line restaurants as well as in smaller ones of high quality. In all but the most conservative, male-dominated kitchens, women have been accepted as equals. Their cuisine is marked by the same flair and skills as that of their male counterparts.

Some examples of outstanding women chefs around the country:

- Jackie Etcheber, owner of Jackie's in Chicago, was recently featured on the PBS "Great Chefs of Chicago." Her Asian- and French-inspired specialties make Jackie's a Chicago favorite.
- Anne Rosenzweig, chef-owner of Arcadia in New York, includes such innovations as chimney-smoked lobster on her menu.
- Cindy Pawlcyn proves that she has business acumen as well as cooking prowess as she juggles the responsibilities of a trio of California restaurants.

Many present-day cooks and chefs originally worked in other fields. One woman was an anthropologist in Africa; another had a wool business. A male chef-owner was once a sales representative for a lawn mower company.

For Aliza Green, owner and executive chef of the trendy Apropos Restaurant in Philadelphia, the preparation of food was a passion from the beginning. A stint of European backpacking was followed by a start as a caterer and experience as a chef with several of Philadelphia's finer restaurants. As head chef of an Italian restaurant, Aliza was responsible for 2,000 meals a week. She was also in charge of buying and approving the food and heading the staff. This small but energetic lady worked seven days a week for two years—a grueling pace for even the most dedicated chef.

Now she's her own boss, with her own restaurant, and she uses her expertise and creativity to the hilt. No shortcuts—in fact, you might say that Aliza takes the long way around. Chocolate is flown in from Europe for baking. Pizzas are prepared in wood-burning ovens to give them a lovely, woodsy taste. With touches such as these, Ms. Green has the pleasure of knowing that her act is going over sensationally.

Benjamin Baskin is a full-fledged chef who has temporarily forsaken the restaurant kitchen to teach cooking classes. When Baskin was a Philadelphia teenager, he started inauspiciously as a dishwasher in a local restaurant. A resident chef at the restaurant took an interest in the young man and showed him how to prepare some of the specialty dishes. Baskin found that he took to the creative part of the restaurant business immediately.

With his career goals established early, Baskin enrolled in the Culinary Institute of America. The graduation diploma became his meal ticket, since it allowed him to work almost anywhere he wished. And indeed, Benjamin Baskin seems to have cooked in just about every desirable place. He was an executive chef at the elegant Petite Marmite in Palm Beach. Florida; an assistant pastry chef in a lovely old Connecticut country inn; and master chef at a restaurant in the Virgin Islands.

Now, Baskin has changed courses and launched into food demonstrations in department stores and on talk shows, and cooking elegant private dinners at people's homes. He also enjoys teaching the skills he has learned over the years in a cooking class setting.

So take note: a chef does not always have to stay with a restaurant or hotel. It is obvious from Baskin's story that a good chef has tremendous opportunities outside the conventional kitchen.

But let's go back to that kitchen a minute and analyze exactly *what* is the best spot for a culinary graduate.

According to *USA Today* (October 29, 1986), established hotel restaurants such as The Restaurant in Houston's Remington Hotel are drawing some of the best talents. Flourishing hotels have the money and resources to offer the new chef a salary and benefits that independent restaurants often cannot equal. According to Patrick Augustyn, Senior Executive Chef for Omni Hotels, a cook out of culinary school may get a starting offer of $14,000 to $18,000 from a privately owned restaurant, but a hotel restaurant may be able to up the ante to $18,000 to $21,000 or more.

According to *USA Today*, the following are a few of the hot spots where newly trained and highly skilled chefs may land the job of their dreams:

Boston:

Restaurant La Marquis de Lafayette
Lafayette Hotel
1 Avenue de Lafayette

Julien
Hotel Meridien
250 Franklin Street

Chicago:

The Ritz-Carlton
160 East Pearson Street

Dallas:

Beau Nash
Crescent Court Hotel
400 Crescent Court

Houston:

The Restaurant
The Remington Hotel
1919 Brier Oaks Lane

Los Angeles:

Colette
Beverly Pavilion Hotel
9360 Wilshire Boulevard

La Chaumière
Century Plaza Hotel
2025 Avenue of the Stars

Miami:

Grand Bay Hotel
2669 South Bayshore Drive

New York:

Cafe Pierre
Hotel Pierre
2 East 61st Street

La Regence
Plaza Athenee
37 East 64th Street

St. Louis:

American Rotisserie
Omni International Hotel
1820 Market Street

San Francisco:

Campton Place
Campton Place Hotel
340 Stockton Street

Stamford, Connecticut:

The Inn at Mill River
26 Mill River Street

Washington, D.C.:

Aux Beaux Champs
Four Seasons Hotel
2800 Pennsylvania Avenue NW

Remember that the trend toward better salaries and greater prestige exists in many hotel chains and individual hotels not on this list.

Not only singles and school graduates venture into the culinary world. Couples—young and older—are buying old farmhouses and unrestored inns as showcases for their cooking expertise. (These are hardly the traditional confines of what one considers a restaurant.)

Michael and Elizabeth Terry are typical of a trend that began in the 1970s. They bought a large, old home in Savannah, Georgia, and converted the first floor into a restaurant (they live in the rest of the mansion). The Terrys' restaurant, Elizabeth's, is truly an American success story, and Elizabeth Terry is ranked as one of the best chefs in the nation.

Michael Terry was an attorney and his wife, a weaver and designer, but Elizabeth's expertise in the kitchen began to take precedence. She received so much praise for her dinner parties that she decided to "go public." She opened a deli in their home town of Atlanta, which was followed by a wine and cheese shop. Later the Terrys moved to Savannah after they had found the perfect house to make into a restaurant. It was a step that nearly tripped up the talented but inexperienced couple.

The kitchen was understaffed, the electricity, erratic, and the dining room, overcrowded. But with Michael's improvements to the place and his role of affable maitre d', Elizabeth's soon became Savannah's favorite restaurant. And his wife's growing reputation as a chef guaranteed future success.

Elizabeth Terry proved she could be one of the best without a formal cooking education. Benjamin Baskin proved he could be at the top with a culinary school diploma. In either case, they were blessed with the skills that make for recognition as outstanding chefs.

Not all the cooking instruction in the world will produce a master chef unless the talent and ambition are there. But if you naturally love to cook, your career decision may almost make itself. And one day, who knows? As a chef, you may develop a "trademark" recipe that earns the ultimate honor: your name as part of its name.

Chapter **VII**

Catering to the Big Moment

If you ask most people what "catering" means, they will probably say, "People bringing food to your house for a special occasion." That is true, but there is another area of catering, one that has grown substantially in recent years. This is catering not *off* the premises, but *on*—at the caterer's own establishment.

Only recently has this form of catering come across as a bonanza business. The reason is simple. The catering business thrives because of today's hectic pace. Many people—especially two-paycheck families with little time to spend in the kitchen—lack the time to plan for events such as christenings and wedding rehearsals (or, for that matter, entire weddings) at home. Such events are scheduled either at the private dining rooms offered by larger restaurants or at a caterer's. Catering establishments are especially prepared to handle every element of a special event.

Trusting these special occasions to "outsiders" has brought many new people into foodservice positions. Chefs and maitre d's, waiters and waitresses, bartenders and bakers shoud check out catering establishments for the opportunities they offer.

A caterer's building could qualify as a restaurant—or two or three! The average caterer's establishment may well have two banquet halls and several rooms for smaller affairs. Such a caterer may host as many as four weddings a day, with an afternoon and evening reception scheduled for each of the two larger rooms. Bar mitzvahs, wedding rehearsal dinners, funeral luncheons, and birthday or anniversary parties may also be taking place in smaller rooms at the same time. Each affair, large or small, is designed to please the hosts and their guests.

The wedding cake awaits the bride and groom at their reception at Presidential Caterers.

Augustus Mandracchia is typical of caterers across the country in his desire to please his customers. Mandracchia, owner of Presidential Caterers in Norristown, Pennsylvania, explains: "My real pleasure is to see people enjoying themelves. These events are big moments in their lives. I want them to remember the warm, friendly service, not just what they had for dinner."

Not that Gus isn't proud of the lavish, tasty banquet choices he offers potential customers. Meeting with the future bride and groom or holiday office party planners, Mandracchia presents a buffet or a "seated" dinner menu. The offerings are lavish, indeed—tables resplendent with well-prepared, colorful foods.

A Presidential wedding buffet would likely include as meats, rounds of beef, veal scallopini, Swedish meatballs, baked Virginia ham, and a whole turkey. Vegetables, casseroles, and dessert sweets are equally diverse and extensive. A carafe of wine might grace each guest table, with champagne for the bridal party at the head table. The Presidential's dinner menu for an office party would be equally generous and planned especially for that kind of event.

Gus Mandracchia sends out a questionnaire after each of his

Who will be the first to sample this elegant swan centerpiece? Creations like these are guaranteed to impress banquet guests at Presidential Caterers.

functions to spot-check every element of the event. Was the service attentive? Was the client pleased with the food? In better than 99 percent of the cases, the host or hostess was delighted, and much of Gus's business is from word-of-mouth recommendations by satisfied customers.

Gus's "conversion rate" of those who contact Presidential Caterers shows how well this attention to detail pays off. A recent eight-month recap of telephone calls showed that 658 potential customers called Presidential, many of them because of its fine reputation. Of these, Gus scheduled 244 appointments, which resulted in 174 catered events. That is a booking rate of 71 percent—a very warming response.

Gus credits much of his success to his handling of "payroll." He is never understaffed, he pays his people well, and he prefers to hire housewives as waitresses for his functions. The housewife, he

Gus Mandracchia, owner of Presidential Caterers, presides at a luau.

feels, sees her job as a way of pleasing others. A person who lavishes care upon her family will devote the same caring attention to the guests she serves. (Gus does hire working waitresses, too, but he looks for that housewifely caring quality in them.)

Prospective caterers are strongly advised not to open an establishment without a large amount of capital.

Fortunately for Gus Mandracchia, initial funding was not a problem. Presidential Caterers was formerly a flourishing restaurant run by his father. When Gus saw the potential of a business devoted exclusively to catering, he persuaded his father to convert the restaurant. His subsequent financial success confirmed his father's trust in him.

Ridgewell Caterers, based in Washington, D.C., claims to be the country's largest off-premises caterer. The company caters nearly 12,000 parties a year, employing 55 bakers and chefs, 250 full-time staff, and 850 waiters-on-call. Its sleek, elegantly lettered trucks can be seen crisscrossing many major cities.

Although Ridgewell Caterers may lead in volume, others set records of a different sort. Pattie Spaziani, a young California caterer, surely takes the cake on unusual party assignments. She has catered in the Amazon, fed a Mick Jagger crowd, and served passengers in a hot-air balloon.

The party for Mick Jagger ended in a run-in with the police. Because she did not have a proper pass, the police wouldn't let Pattie deliver her refreshments. The order—1,200 sundaes rapidly becoming 1,200 milkshakes—forced a split-second decision: She rammed the closed gates of the Los Angeles Coliseum with police cars in hot pursuit. Jagger and his groupies got the sundaes. The police pressed no charges (and got in on the desserts.)

Another unforgettable event for Pattie was the hot-air balloon dinner. The idea blossomed from a friend's request to do something romantic for his girlfriend's birthday. So a candlelit dinner it was; the "candles," of course, were battery-charged. Pattie played the part of waitress in the flight, serving the couple wine, scampi, and scallops. The setting sun provided the ideal backdrop to the adventure.

Pattie offers services to *huge* numbers of guests. She once catered a trade show in San Francisco for 6,000 people. The func-

To enhance the Hawaiian theme, leis decorate the wine fountain at the festive banquet hosted by Presidential Caterers.

tion consisted of six ongoing menus, ranging from spicy Mexican fare to delicate Chinese specialties.

Affairs such as these require tremendous amounts of equipment, including everything from champagne fountains to tablecloths. Pattie's catering establishment, besides storing all this party equipment, houses two giant walk-in refrigerators, an eight-burner stove with double ovens, and a huge convection oven. A staff of 100 people keeps the place humming.

Catering off-premises (as well as in-house) has its share of drama, as Pattie or any other caterer will tell you. Ludwig Bemelmans, a writer who was also an experienced hotelier, once said of parties and banquets: "It is very important that absolutely nothing goes wrong. If the last and least important guest is offended by an employee, thinks he is being neglected, or finds a piece of china or a splinter of bone in his soup, then the entire party is ruined. The host will forget all that has been good about it and only mention the bad."

Large-scale caterers are not the only people who bring near-perfect efficiency and creativity to their work. Home-based caterers also set high standards for themselves. Many home caterers work full-time supplying local restaurants or private customers with top-quality food.

Fran Accetta, of Chestnut Hill, Pennsylvania, and her partner, Pat Bassetti, are skilled cooks who prefer to keep their operation small-scale. It didn't take too much time for their Tasty Tea Sandwiches service to take hold. Word spread rapidly that these two ladies made delicious and reasonably priced hors d'oeuvres.

" 'Word-of-mouth' is certainly a prime way to rustle up orders," Fran Accetta explains. "But there are other ways, too. You can develop a mailing list from your satisfied customers, letting them know that you'd like to serve them again." Also, Fran adds, "try to get orders from churches, corporations, and other organizations. Once you have catered their parties, they'll make your services a habit." Mrs. Accetta also advocates advertising in the local newspapers.

Fran and Pat do their marketing two days before the orders must be delivered. The following day, they make the fillings for the sandwiches. On delivery day, they assemble from one hundred to five hundred sandwiches per order, using assembly-line methods.

Tasty Tea Sandwiches knows its limitations. "We seldom do back-to-back orders," Fran says. "If we tried to fill orders three days in a row, the quality of our food would suffer and we wouldn't be in such good shape ourselves."

How profitable is a small catering business? "It's a nice supplement to the income," Fran explains, "but it's not something to count on. Holidays can be very profitable, but other times of the year are often very lean."

One thing is for sure: Bigger profits do not come from cutting food costs. "Never buy inferior foods," Fran cautions. "You may increase your profit temporarily, but your orders are bound to diminish."

The best answer is to get the finest products at cost. This seeming contradiction—best quality at bottom dollar—is possible if you are willing to shop around.

Fran and Pat *do* go out of their way to make a superior product. They work as a team, crediting part of their success to their very organized approach. But their relationship goes beyond teamwork. They are good friends who laugh, chat, and reminisce as they work together in Fran's large, sunny kitchen. "Working with a good friend is part of the pleasure of a catering business," Fran explains. "Time passes quickly when you are elbow-deep in tuna salad—as long as you have someone you like to work with."

The other great and obvious pleasure of a catering business is working with food. Caterers regard their work as an art as well as a science. The precise measurement of ingredients, the careful cooking of the various foods, and the final preparations are transformed into delectable decorations. The caterer's greatest pleasure is to please the eye as well as the palate.

Chapter *VIII*

(Almost) Everyone's Dream: Opening a Restaurant

For many people the thought of opening a restaurant is irresistible. The foodservice graduate and the restaurant professional often consider restaurant ownership the ultimate goal. Even the doctor, lawyer, merchant, and housewife dream of renovating old farmhouses and opening them as inns. Or the 9-to-5 office worker fantasizes the corner pub as a mini-gourmet eatery where he or she can work independently and creatively.

The idea of opening a restaurant, although universally appealing, is often too much to handle. Those without experience and finances are advised to research the field carefully before they plunge ahead. Even those experienced in the business may find running a restaurant frustrating and ultimately unsuccessful. For instance, a thriving and charming Pennsylvania restaurant recently went out of business because the capable owners could not get neighbors to agree to their application for a liquor license. Despite daily "full houses," the operating expenses were overwhelming. The sale of liquor would have helped the restaurant turn a profit.

The sad truth is that most restaurants fail. Lack of experience, insufficient financing, unwillingness to commit to long hours, and poor location are among the factors that make this a tough business.

But despite the high dropout rate, there *are* successful restaurants. Yours can be among them if you heed the advice of lawyers, realtors, and current restaurateurs. Their experience will put you way ahead on your project.

An overwhelming interest in food is an essential ingredient of successful restaurant ownership. Food preparation should be a favorite activity as well as a way of making money. And along with this, the future restaurant owner must have 24-hour energy and a strong, outgoing personality.

If you are serious about starting a restaurant, think of yourself as a stage producer, director, actor, and set designer all in one (perhaps a costumer, too). Your stage, of course, is your restaurant.

As producer, you bring together all the elements including the finances. As designer, you create the scenery, the decor of your restaurant. It must reflect your personality and uniqueness. You also write, or co-author, the three-act (or five-course) script, the menu. Finally, you direct a small or large cast, depending on the size of your staff. Think of chef, sous-chef, dessert chef, and bartender as your leading actors; waiters, buspeople, and cashier as your supporting players and stagehands. Unlike the real theater, your "curtain" may rise early—your performance may begin well before noon and continue until long after midnight. And your successful "run" may last for years.

This is all a tall order, but it can be accomplished if certain basics are observed. Be sure you have an adequate business background as well as experience in restaurant management. You should be familiar with such specialty areas as quantity cooking, inventory control, and menu planning.

Your most important function will be to plan the dishes you will serve in your restaurant. The menu must express *you*, of course, but it also has to meet the needs of the community. If you offer a meal that is too adventurous for the area, you may fail to attract the customers you need in those first crucial days. Later, if you wish, you can introduce some of your more creative ideas while maintaining your popularity with local favorite dishes.

Menu planning is not just the choice of interesting recipes and the magic touch of the chef. Meal preparation also includes the intricacies of food pricing. If you don't have expertise in this area, find someone who does. There are formulas that must be followed or your profit will be as slim as an empty doggie bag. Such formulas for profit-making must take into consideration food delivery, food storage, and salaries for the chef, food servers, and other staff, plus such overhead costs as rent or mortgage, taxes, and utilities.

Location is *crucial* to success. That does not mean that you have to have an eye-catching building in the best part of town. It *does* mean that your restaurant site should be a practical, appealing one. It should encompass every desirable feature from easy parking to a safe neighborhood and the presence of other businesses.

When considering restaurant sites, also familiarize yourself with the codes, ordinances, and licenses you will need to open your doors. Short of telling you what you may serve, codes literally police your restaurant life. Fire codes, health regulations, trash disposal methods, and sewer codes, although cumbersome and pesky, keep your restaurant a welcome neighbor. That goes, too, for liquor laws, if they apply in your case.

There is a question, too, of whether to buy a building already fitted out as a restaurant or to start with an empty shell. Generally, it makes sense to buy a building operating as a restaurant because it requires less remodeling. But you should investigate fully to find out why the restaurant is available. Did it fail? If so, was the failure related to the operation itself or to location factors that would doom any restaurant? Make sure the reason for sale is reasonable, such as the owner's desire to retire. Don't learn too late that a four-lane highway is going to back up on your future restaurant!

Whether you take over an existing restaurant or start from scratch, you will need two savvy people: a real estate agent and a lawyer. The real estate agent must be experienced in advising potential restaurant owners—or at least be familiar with selling and renting commercial real estate. The lawyer should have some expertise in the restaurant business, to protect your interests when it comes to the fine print of restaurant leases or agreements of sale.

Of course, you must be sure you have the funds for a place before you even consider renting or buying it. If major financing is coming from a bank, the banker must feel certain that you can repay the loan. Keep in mind that banks are rarely willing to lend money for new restaurants. As one start-your-own-restaurant book says, "Enthusiasm and pride of ownership are not considered a form of capital!" But if you are certain you can swing it financially, there are several ways to fund your project. One is through debt financing; another, equity financing. Any book on financing a business will cover these and other methods in detail. Here, too, your attorney may be extremely helpful, in giving you financing advice, and possibly in finding suitable sources of funds—perhaps partners or investors.

Many things must be considered in determining your financial needs. They run the gamut from per-square-foot rental costs to paying staff salaries. Other considerations include the purchase of kitchen equipment. Restaurant auctions are a good source of reasonably priced kitchen equipment. Leasing the equipment is another possibility.

You must also have a realistic idea of your costs in relation to profits. For instance, you can figure out the price of your average meal by computing menu costs. Menu costs reflect not only your marketing bill, but your entire restaurant operation. Figured into the cost of each meal must be everything from the chef, staff, and advertising to repayment of principal and interest on any bank loan, plus your everyday overhead.

Once you're secure about financing, you can concentrate on some of the more pleasant aspects of restaurant ownership—the building's design, or dining room decor, as an example. To create a practical yet eye-catching restaurant, you must find an architect who is compatible. If the architect envisions floor-to-ceiling mirrors and dazzling lights, and you favor dark paneling and candles, your working relationship is bound to be tense.

While you determine the restaurant's style and decor, you will also want to assemble your staff. Next to food, staff is the most important consideration for the new owner. *Staff* is not just cook and waiter (except for very small establishments where a few people do many jobs), but buspeople, bartenders, the maitre d', dishwashers, and all the other employees who make a restaurant run smoothly.

Restaurant workers can be among your more unusual types. After all, as one owner put it, "What normal person would work in often hectic conditions, at hours exhausting and irregular enough to produce jet-lag?" A restaurant baker, for instance, often bakes all night and sleeps all day.

The restaurant owner, then, presides over a panoply of personalities, now soothing, now encouraging them—sometimes even scolding them. A restaurant is run somewhat like a benevolent army; the general must inspire respect and obedience from the troops. The many successful restaurants across the country exist because of effective management combined with affirmative "people" attitudes—positive ways of viewing staff and customers alike.

When you train your staff, you will want to instill those qualities that will mold exceptional workers. Your staff's positive response to your training will pay off in many ways. They will remain with you as fellow players in your restaurant's success. Careless training or indifferent treatment, on the other hand, will lead to rapid turnover—a definite drain on your profits and a strain on your reputation.

One of the most effective ways to retain your staff is to be able to do everything they do—prepare an omelet, fix a clogged drain, and set a proper table. Your expertise—and willingness—will set an example and encourage your staff to work hard for you.

Now, as opening day approaches for your restaurant, you will have established routines that will make business run smoothly. Your staff will have the place blindingly clean. Your pantry and refrigerators will be filled to exactly the degree that will meet your needs yet avoid food spoilage and waste. In pre-opening food preparation runs, you've sampled and approved (or rejected!) all of the many dishes your chef and assistants will prepare. You've spotted the wilted lettuce, the too-garlicky sauce before your new customers can.

Tonight, you'll welcome the dining community for the first time. The serving steps you and your staff have been rehearsing will appear to be instinctive. Your maitre d' or hostess will give undivided attention to arriving customers. Your waiters will know when each diner is ready for the next course. If you run out of some dishes early, you'll know which buying habits to change. Naturally, a few things will go wrong; still, you will most likely feel very good about your debut as a restaurateur.

As you enter your second or third week in business, you will want to make a sales count—a computation that will show which menu items are selling and which are not. Taking unpopular items off the menu is like lightening a plane's deadweight; your restaurant will "fly" better with a popular menu.

* * *

Most successful restaurants have followed these ABCs of restaurant ownership. Caroline's, a small, new restaurant in Philadelphia, is an excellent case history. The owner, Bill Hoffman, makes this chapter come to life as he deals with the exciting but exacting details that accompany a restaurant's creation.

Hoffman's restaurant credentials were impressive; an extensive culinary background and previous restaurant management experience. Because of this training he was equipped to meet the challenges and stresses of owning and running a restaurant.

Bill debated his restaurant's location, consulted and drew up plans with his architect, and wrestled with budget decisions. He found that he needed $375,000 as working capital. He and a junior partner, chef David Raimon, secured this large sum through bank loans, investments from stockholders—and by scavenging Bill's own pockets!

Once the money was assured, they began site-looking. Hoffman and Raimon found a place that met all their requirements. It was in an attractive part of town, bound to draw affluent customers from the surrounding neighborhood. As one restaurant reviewer later wrote: "Caroline's is in a high-density area, a solid gridlock of some of the most desirable traffic in town."

Because this was to be a "neighborhood" restaurant, the young owner wanted his place to have a comfortable feeling. Hoffman remembered his grandmother's welcoming kitchen-dining room, and he wanted his customers to enjoy that same homey atmosphere. He was able to recreate this ambiance, spending some $42,000 of his $375,000 investment on the dining room decor.

The welcoming, neighborhood feeling also permeates the $29,000 bar. With its wallpaper featuring teapots and ivy leaves, it is a refreshing change from the cool-colors-and-chrome-plate look of many bars.

Even with their hefty financing, the restaurant team ran out of money a month before they were due to open. The only way to begin generating a return on everyone's investment was to open

Caroline's earlier than Hoffman would have liked. And, on the night they opened, they were so hard up for cash that they had to borrow money to put into the cash register! Nor was the place ready for "company." The electricians remained, wiring ciruits right up to the last minute, the place reeked of glue—and the kitchen ran out of hot water.

Despite these opening jitters, the location, decor, and attractive food pricing of Caroline's paid off for Hoffman. In fact, the new owner had a flyaway success on his hands. Caroline's was filled to capacity every night.

Bill Hoffman, now almost a year into his business, still ". . .cannot believe that it has all worked out so well." Let us hope that when you open your restaurant, you too will enjoy the same good fortune.

Chapter IX

Learning the Job with a Flair

Years ago, you went to Paris for your schooling if you wanted to learn serious cooking. When you had completed the culinary curriculum, you then returned to America and sought employment in one of the country's exclusive restaurants or hotels.

Today, you do not need to cross the ocean to learn haute cuisine or spend years waiting on tables while you take restaurant management courses part time. You can receive equivalent schooling at one of the special culinary schools in this country. These schools can also prepare you for restaurant management if you prefer overseeing a restaurant rather than cooking for one. Tuition is high and the work demanding, but the results are worth the time and money. The proof is in the pudding—or the Beef Wellington, or the Baked Alaska. These and the skills necessary to create such delicacies make you a valuable commodity.

Whether the talent is in your head or your hands, you graduate certified in your field. In many cases you may receive an Associate in Specialized Business degree. This fully accredited degree is recognized by the National Association of Trade and Technical Schools. Graduating chefs and pastry chefs are awarded a diploma attesting to their competence in food and pastry preparation.

The Restaurant School in Philadelphia was the first in the country to train people in the art of operating small, high-quality restaurants. Built on the belief that "Great Restaurants Aren't Born...They're Graduated," the school combines practical experience with formal education. The three programs offered include Restaurant Management, Chef Training, and the Pastry

Chef program. Each course lasts approximately one year and prepares the graduate for immediate work.

The Restaurant School curriculum recognizes that restaurant owners and managers prefer to hire people who are fully trained. Since the restaurant business is not purely academic, the school also believes that a four-year college degree is not necessary; its shorter, accelerated courses provide the practical skills needed for success. (There are also programs that include an all-expenses-paid week-long culinary program in France!)

The Restaurant School is typical of the special schools in its careful student selection. Although foodservice experience is helpful, many graduates have come to the school from other fields.

At The Restaurant School, students learn by doing: in this case the basics of fresh vegetable preparation.

What all students have in common is a love of fine food and high motivation to learn lifetime skills. One of the most important parts of each student's application—and the basis for the in-depth interview that comes before acceptance—is the Goal Statement. It is phrased this way on the application: "Please write a statement of your goals as they relate to your career and how you plan to meet them. This statement should be a minimum of one hundred fifty words." The school also asks students to list "five important elements that you consider necessary in having a successful restaurant." This thorough screening of potential students plus the detailed, intensive instruction gives the school an enviable 92 percent foodservice placement rate for its graduates.

Future pastry chefs create exquisite "homework" like this at The Restaurant School.

The school's Restaurant Management Program is its most extensive—a 12-month curriculum with 1,710 clock hours' training, 72 academic credits earned, and an Associate in Specialized Business degree awarded. Total tuition, $7,600. As with all Restaurant School programs, grants, loans, and other forms of student aid are available.

The Restaurant Management Program offers courses in business managment, culinary arts, dining room service, bar management, wine service, marketing, computer technology, conversatioal French, human resources, business law, and principles of business operation. Practical training takes place in the school's own—and very popular—Philadelphia restaurant under the guidance of a full faculty.

Two forms of the Chef Training Program are offered, full and part time. Both award diplomas upon graduation. The part-time program is geared to the student who is working—perhaps in the restaurant field. The full-time program takes 8½ months (923 clock hours), while the part-time program spreads its 924 clock hours over 62 weeks. Tuition for either program: $6,500.

The Chef Training Program covers every area of food preparation and kitchen management. Students build their cooking efficiency one class at a time, advancing from knife skills through sauces, soups, salads, vegetables, seafood, poultry, meats, and game to pastry and desserts. Classroom work is followed by an apprenticeship in one of Philadelphia's finer kitchens. Chef Training graduates are ready to work as sous chef, first cook, kitchen manager—perhaps as full chef, depending on previous experience, school training, and initiative.

The Pastry Chef Program at the Restaurant School is conducted in the European tradition, in which artistry is as much an ingre-

A dessert is prepared at tableside by a student of The Restaurant School. The school's restaurant is open to the public.

dient as are flour and sugar. Time and tuition for the Pastry Chef Program differ from the Chef's Program.

Master patissiers (or pastry chefs) teach students the basics of doughs, mousses, creams, frozen desserts, confectionery, and chocolates. Students then advance to elaborate decorative work, a review of general kitchen procedures, and courses in business and retail management. A diploma is awarded for this comprehensive course of study. Graduates are ready for work in pastry shops, catering businesses, restaurants, or perhaps even on cruise ships.

Gene and Phyllis Gosfield were ready to start a small restaurant after graduating from the Restaurant School. They found the school's training in this area invaluable, according to Gene.

Seated in one of the charming rooms of the Gosfields' Under

Students learn the fine points of wine service in this class at The Restaurant School.

the Blue Moon Restaurant in Chestnut Hill, Pennsylvania, Gene affirmed the value of his culinary background. "There is no way we could have been successful without our Restaurant School training. The school set standards for excellence that stay with me to this day," says the 1976 graduate.

From the beginning, Gene was interested in the "up-front" work. His role as maitre d' perfectly fits his personality. His pleasure in his guests, dry sense of humor, and skill at handling the myriad chores of such a job reflect a perfect blend of his personality and school training. His wife, Phyllis, an excellent cook long before her professional training, took over the culinary end of things.

"Our Maitre d' Professor was an Austrian with impeccable credentials," Gosfield explains. "He and the others on the staff advised, scolded, made us question, *shaped* us into professionals."

The fact that Under the Blue Moon has set standards for fine food in a town of top-quality restaurants attests to the excellence of the Restaurant School training.

Another prestigious cooking school is the Culinary Institute of America, in Hyde Park, New York. Graduates of the Institute move rapidly into key culinary positions in this country and throughout the world.

Tuition and fees are high, but the unique curriculum justifies the cost. The total package for 21 months in residence averages some $12,700. Financial aid is available, as it is at most major culinary schools in the United States.

The Institute's degree of Associate in Occupational Studies is affirmation of a student's competency in cooking, baking, and restaurant management. The degree is earned by completing a series of curriculum "blocks" ranging from mastery of seafood cookery to introductory dining room service.

A sample block, Culinary Skill Development II, is a 55-hour, 1½-credit course that encompasses vegetable cookery, meat, fish, and poultry cooking. Basic techniques such as sautéeing, roasting, poaching, braising, and frying are included in the course.

The faculty credentials are awesome (as are those of the teaching staff of The Restaurant School). As an example, Paul Prosperi, the Culinary Institute's Baking/Pastry Chef Instructor, was educated at the Ministère de l'Education Nationale in France. He served his apprenticeship at the Bourbonneux Pastry Shop in Paris. His professional experience includes employment at Les Delices and Fauchon in Paris and Fortnum and Mason's in London. He has won the Grand Prize for classical pastry at the Salon of Culinary Arts in New York City, two gold medals from the Société Culinaire Philanthropique, and numerous other medals. Monsieur Prosperi's colleagues have achieved similar recognition.

Other highly recommended cooking schools are found throughout the country. They are of many specialties and sizes, and their counterparts are found in the major cities of Europe.

The International Association of Cooking Professionals, the

The Restaurant Management Program at The Restaurant School leads to the degree of Associate in Specialized Business, an excellent stepping-stone to a variety of foodservice careers. The computer helps to plan meals and budgets.

"voice" of the cooking school industry, publishes the "Directory of Institutional Members," which lists all the IACP-accredited cooking schools in the United States and Europe. It can be purchased from the Association for $3.75; write to 1001 Connecticut Avenue NW, Washington, DC 20036.

An example of a foreign school listing is the Ballymaloe Cookery School in County Cork, Ireland. During year-round instruction, the school offers catering, celebrity chef instruction, and Chinese, Mid-East, and Nouvelle Cookery.

At home the listed schools range from the extremely prestigious L'Academie de Cuisine in Bethesda, Maryland, to smaller enterprises such as Gourmet Gadgetre, Ltd., in Oklahoma City, Oklahoma. The descriptions are quite detailed, such as that for La Venture in Skokie, Illinois. Cited are its year-round, part-time, and full-time course schedules, including training in breadmaking, catering, Chinese, French, and Italian cooking, chocolate and pastry specialties, and confection and decorating courses.

The directory offers suggestions on what to look for in a school, whether you choose one in their listing or an unlisted but perhaps equally proficient institution that has not sought IACP accreditation. It suggests that you look for a school that accents technique, the principles of cooking, rather than initial preparation of dishes. It also suggests classes in which you can participate. *Knead* the dough; don't just watch someone else doing it. Find out if the teacher gives homework—a salad or dessert to prepare. (Here's one time your family will *encourage* you to do your homework!) Inspect the school. Is it roomy enough to allow a number of people to move about comfortably from countertop to stove? If the place you are considering fulfills these and other criteria, you are likely to have a rewarding school experience.

Anyone currently engaged in full-time culinary study is eligible for membership in the Association at the Student/Apprentice level. Members receive the Association newsletter, consumer information on food-related subjects, introductions to leading food, wine, and cooking-related companies or headquarters offering information, and member "networking." The Association regularly updates the directory, adding new listings of both large and small cooking schools.

A word on these small cooking schools (and those not listed by the IACP): They are widespread. There are at least fifty in Philadelphia and its suburbs alone. They often specialize, offering in-depth courses in Chinese cooking, vegetarian cookery, and ethnic menus. There is also a strong emphasis on health-oriented cuisine such as macrobiotic cookery.

The small, intimate schools can help you in two ways. They can train you in specialized cooking in an informal atmosphere, and you can learn the basics of running a small cooking school yourself by observing their methods.

The small but dedicated cooking schools as well as our country's major culinary institutes reflect the spirit and performance of the entire foodservice industry today. Their proliferation also reflects the country's love affair with good food.

Chapter **X**

Landing a Job in Foodservice

There's a job for almost everyone in foodservice, America's Number One employer. With that banner news, we can move ahead to your goals. This chapter will be helpful to you whether you are interested in finding an entry-level job in foodservice or are aiming for a high-level position such as restaurant manager.

Entry-level positions require a minimum of training. The responsibilities of busboy or busgirl, waiter or waitress, or fast-food server are usually learned on the job.

Middle-level jobs usually require some experience. Among the more responsible positions in this category are cashier, cook, bartender, meat cutter, and purchasing agent.

"Top-rung" assignments include dining room manager, director of recipe development, and executive chef. These are the industry's key positions and the long-term goals of the culinary or foodservice management student.

Besides ample career opportunities, the foodservice industry allows mobility within the field. Because of high turnover, you can move from one type of work—or one geographic area—to another fairly easily. Foodservice is also the field where women and minoritics find exceptional employment breaks. In the industry as a whole, 64.8 percent of all workers are women, and 13.8 percent belong to minorities.

So, the jobs are there. Now, how do you find them?

The National Institute for the Foodservice Industry advises you to check your local newspaper want-ads, trade journal classified sections, and job placement centers, some of which specialize in foodservice careers.

The Institute also suggests that you talk to people in foodservice work. Many of them know where the jobs are. And if you are still in high school and looking for a job, your guidance counselors and school placement officers may be very helpful.

Private and state employment services may also be able to give you leads. Private employment services for middle- or executive-level jobs may charge a fee for placement, but they save job-hunting time. State employment services often offer the same services, and they are free.

If you are already in a position of responsibility but want to change jobs within the industry, rely on *inside* information. The food salesmen and women who come to your restaurant are brokers or "middlemen" for foods and beverages, and they often know where the jobs are. As in every career area, news travels fast within the field.

Interviews and résumés are necessary for foodservice positions as they are in any profession. Résumés are generally not needed for entry-level jobs in the fast-food chains, but there may be a biographical sheet to fill out when applying for a job. Interviews, however, are definitely a part of the hiring process for such places as McDonald's or Taco Bell (see Chapter II for more on the interview process and fast-food outlets).

The résumé you will need for middle- and upper-level jobs can be as helpful to you as it is to the potential employer. A résumé can help you organize your thoughts about your future. It may even determine the type of foodservice work you want to do. Are you interested mostly in food preparation? Perhaps restaurant management? Maybe maitre d' appeals to you, with its opportunities for direct contact with the public.

Basically, your résumé lets people know what you have done and what you want to do. If you send it to a prospective employer before your interview, it can serve as an introduction and make it easier for both of you to cover those points that are already down on paper.

It helps to attach a cover letter to your résumé. Be sure to find out the name of your prospective employer or the personnel manager so that you an open the letter with "Dear Mr. Jones" or "Dear Miss Davis," for example, instead of "Dear Sir." Also, mention the interview dates that would fit in with your schedule. This mailing should be followed by a phone call to find out what day and hour would be convenient for the interview.

Your chances of being hired are greater if you know something about the company. Recruiters will be flattered if you do some homework on the business. Your letter will be stronger if it reflects this knowledge, and your interview will be more enjoyable.

Remember that dressing well counts, and being on time for the interview tells the employer you'll be punctual on the job, too.

You are welcome to ask a prospective employer questions, even encouraged to do so. "What are my duties?" will certainly be one of your first questions. "How will I be paid?" "What are my opportunities for advancement?" Answers to these questions will give you a clearer understanding of the job.

As you leave, you can end the interview in an upbeat way with comments such as: "I'd really like to work for you. I like this place." Spoken with sincerity, your words make an impression.

When you land your foodservice job, you may be surprised at its benefit package. Because the industry wants to be competitive with other industries, you may find yourself with advantages you didn't expect. Many organizations offer health and accident benefits. Some have retirement plans. Paid vacations may expand with your time on the job.

In the end, however, your most valuable benefit may be that you are in an industry that allows you to locate wherever you wish and work in a specialty area that appeals to you.

Chapter **XI**

All About Culinary Education and Financial Aid

Many people learn about cooking or restaurant management by working their way up the foodservice ladder. But a faster way to reach the top is through education in the field. The stronger your educational background, the greater your opportunity to land a challenging job. Whether you take advantage of culinary courses in a vo-tech high school, programs in junior college, opportunities while in military service, or attendance at a culinary school or four-year college, you will acquire knowledge that would otherwise often be gained in a haphazard way. The four-year college program and the major culinary schools are, of course, the most desirable because of their intensive approach to food-service education.

But junior and community colleges are also fast becoming entrées to important food positions. By offering in-depth study of the various phases of foodservice, they can graduate students who are ready to go to work. The two-year college with its associate degree often provides an excellent culinary background.

Four years in college and a bachelor's degree in restaurant management qualify you for a top position in the field, or at least one where your apprenticeship will be short. This is even more true for the culinary school graduate who becomes a chef. Food-service people who hire graduates are putting fully trained people into demanding jobs.

But perhaps college graduation is a far distant goal. If you are about to enter high school, you want to know what you can do *now* with your interest in a culinary career. You can get a head start in the field if you are in a nonspecialized high school with foodservice

77

electives or a vo-tech school offering a foodservice curriculum. (For career information and a directory of accredited trade and technical schools, write to the National Association of Trade and Technical Schools, 2251 Wisconsin Avenue NW, Washington, DC 20070.)

The Mastbaum Vocational and Technical High School in Philadelphia is typical of the many vo-tech schools across the country that offer a solid experience in cooking or restaurant operation. Mastbaum students learn to cook, bake, help with the shopping, plan the menus, and wait on tables.

The teachers at Mastbaum High School have a special reason to look forward to their lunch hour: Their meals are prepared by the students in the school's foodservice program. Their diligence and creativity make lunch time a gourmet-time for the teachers, many of them the students' food instructors.

According to food theory teacher Leonard DeFinis, the Mastbaum foodservice program puts the youngsters way ahead of

At the Mastbaum Vo-Tech High School in Philadelphia, while two students check out the container storage units...

...boys and girls prepare the day's meal.

ordinary graduates wishing to go into the restaurant business. "Our program gives them a head start," says DeFinis. It also accustoms them to handling the inevitable complaints connected with food preparation. A teacher or staff member, for instance, complains about a dish being served lukewarm in the school cafeteria. The complaint then goes through the chain of command. The waiter or waitress relays the information to the student manager, who consults with the kitchen staff. The offending dish, this time properly warmed, is quickly forthcoming.

The skills learned at Mastbaum often translate into after-school jobs. One student works with dietitians at a hospital. Another helps a local caterer. There is no doubt that foodservice students from *this* high school are thoroughly at home in the restaurant, the dining room, or behind the scenes in the kitchen.

But the Mastbaum Vo-Tech High School is not the only place in Philadelphia to gain culinary experience. Other schools offer courses in the fields.

Salads get special touches...

If there is no high school near you with programs such as those in the Philadelphia schools, you should plan to work in a food-service operation during summer vacations or in a part-time job during the school year. You will soon know if you enjoy working in the food industry. If you like foodservice work, tell the management. If your bosses know your interests go beyond a summer paycheck, they may give you greater responsibility and more variety.

Many community and junior colleges offer programs designed to place students in foodservice positions immediately upon graduation. (See the Appendix for a list of junior and community colleges.) Montgomery County Community College outside Philadelphia is one such school. It offers two degrees in the culinary field, Hospitality Management in Foodservice, and Hospitality Management in Lodgings. Each associate degree involves approximately 30 semester hours.

The Hospitality Management in Foodservice program is designed to prepare the graduate for entry-level foodservice management. This includes the business skills needed to make mangagement decisions. Here is the course roster for the four semesters (two years):

First Semester	Credit Hours
English Composition I	3
Math or Data Processing Elective	3
Quantity Food Purchasing	3
Introduction to the Hospitality Industry	3
Management of Food and Beverage Service	3
	15

Second Semester	Credit Hours
Psychology of Human Relations in Business	3
Accounting Principles I	3
Hospitality Management Practicum I	1
Food and Beverage Cost Controls	3
Maintenance Management for Hospitality Facilities	3
Physical Education Elective	2
	15

Third Semester	Credit Hours
Introduction to Speech Communication	3
Social Relations Elective	3
Hospitality Management Practicum II	1
Food Production Management I	4
Hospitality Marketing Management	3
	15

Fourth Semester	Credit Hours
History Elective	3
English Elective	3
Business Elective	3
Food Production Management II	4
Hospitality Management Techniques	3
	16

...and potatoes are sliced for a side dish.

Whereas community colleges offer courses leading to entry-level management positions, four-year college students majoring in hospitality and foodservice are preparing to be general managers, banquet managers, and food purchasing agents, among other jobs.

The industry has plenty of room for food management graduates. It also welcomes newly graduated chefs. This warm reception is partly the result of the growing popularity of dining out as well as revolutionary changes in the American life-style. The retirement-home community is one of those changes. Older

The hard work in the kitchen produces a delicious soup for customers

people who once lived with their children or on their own are now moving into "villages" that offer dining facilities, health care, and other services. This shift in living patterns has created thousands of positions for chefs and restaurant managers.

A retirement community's advertisement in a Philadelphia newspaper is typical of those underscoring good food as an attraction for would-be residents. Cathedral Village, "distinguished for its services to residents," according to the advertisement, announced that its chef has a Bachelor of Science in Culinary Arts degree from Johnson and Wales College in Rhode Island. This

This young man tallies up a meal.

is good news to senior citizens considering Cathedral Village as their home—or who are already there. As they head toward the Village's dining room, they can count on good quality and attractiveness in each meal.

Few four-year colleges offer degrees in culinary arts. (These are more the province of two-year colleges and culinary schools). Generally, bachelor's degrees are awarded in HRIM (Hotel, Restaurant and Institutional Management) programs. As the title implies, these curricula offer management training in all areas of hospitality, including those not related to food.

But HRIM programs *do* have hands-on cooking classes among the many courses they offer. The proportion of cooking classes to management courses depends on the composition of the faculty at a given college. If the faculty is more cooking-related, the catalog or course list will reflect that slant.

Drexel University in Philadelphia is one of the many universities and colleges offering the HRIM program. (HRIM programs across the country vary with each college. There is no across-the-board curriculum.) The four-year course of study leads to a bachelor of science degree. The University also offers a co-op program, placing students in a professional setting that complements their studies.

William J. Burt, program coordinator for the Drexel food-services program, feels that the best restaurant and hotel managers

KATHY IVANS PHOTO

Two HRIM majors enjoy whipping up a dish in the culinary science lab at Drexel University.

are those who have worked in a variety of positions in the field. While on co-op, for instance, those in food management may work in the restaurant manager's accounting office, where they learn the very serious business of making a profit.

The Drexel University catalog states that its program "is designed to prepare graduates for a career in hospitality management in restaurants, luxury hotels, lodging chains, resorts, casinos, convention centers, colleges and universities, business and industrial cafeterias, caterers and multi-unit chains."

The Drexel curriculum ranges from courses in the chemical and physical properties of food to units on the serving of food in quantity. The in-depth approach to the subject of food is evident in courses such as Nutrition II. This class offers "the principles of human nutrition, energy metabolism, carbohydrates, lipids, proteins, minerals and vitamins."

"Lipids" and "metabolism" may seem remote from the dynamics of maitre d' training, but a rounded curriculum makes for a better qualified graduate. Drexel University and other colleges consider that their primary goal.

As an HRIM graduate from a four-year college, what can you expect to draw as salary? Not as much as an accounting or a computer graduate. The HRIM graduate earns $19,000 to $20,000 against the accounting graduate's $24,000. But in two years the restaurant-management graduate may be making $30,000 to $35,000 because of the bonus system many eating establishments offer. The accounting graduate usually cannot hope to advance by such leaps and bounds.

But the students' awareness of their marketability can be a drawback. New HRIM graduates tend to be overconfident and impatient to reach the top. Campus job recruiters complain that new Culinary Arts and Restaurant Management graduates want to become general managers of hotels before the ink on the college diploma is dry! This may be because they have served off-campus in positions of great responsibility as students. They have a degree of self-assurance that graduating students in other fields cannot always claim.

However, the aspiring "general·manager" is going to have to wait a few years and accept the responsibilities of his or her

As part of her co-op program, a Drexel University HRIM major serves as hostess at the Hilton Hotel in Philadelphia.

present position. In time, the title may fall in place when the employee is big enough for the job.

An education in the culinary arts or in restaurant management can be as costly as instruction in any other field. To offset some of the costs, it's best to pursue the student loan route. Check out the scholarship and other financial aid available at the college, university, or culinary school you plan to attend. Many major cultinary-arts and restaurant-management schools offer excellent financial aid packages.

The food industry itself has made an investment in foodservice students through scholarship and grant programs. A financial aid program is administered by the National Institute for the Foodservice Industry. Also available are the NIFI-Heinz Scholarship programs, the IFMA (International Foodservice Manufacturers Association) Gold Plate Scholarship porgram, and the NIFI-

National Restaurant Association Teacher Work-Study Grant program. (The latter is strictly for educators working in the field.)

The NIFI-Heinz Scholarships are supported by the H.J. Heinz Company Foundation and include financial help in junior and four-year colleges. The Foundation also offers fellowships to foodservice educators.

The NIFI and IFMA Gold Plate Scholarships are awarded to foodservice management students in junior and four-year colleges. For information on these programs, write to:

> National Institute for the Foodservice Industry
> 20 North Wacker Drive
> Chicago, IL 60606

In your inquiry letter, say that you are interested in all available financial aid programs.

While scholarship aid is helpful, you can also earn money for college by working in any aspect of the foodservice industry. And while you work as waiter or waitress, fast-foods manager or summertime chef, take a few mental notes. What things do you like about where you work? What improvements would you suggest? How would you run the place if it were yours? Those mental notes may come in handy in the future when you wear an executive chef's hat or mange a major food franchise. Your future in foodservice can start *now*. So can the rewards, in this outgoing, attractive profession.

Chapter XII

What's New in the Restaurant Industry?

The world of food is becoming more exciting than ever. Restaurants are growing, fast-food places are at every commercial turn of the road; catering and foodservice have become more imaginative. That's because Americans like to *eat*—and now, they like special touches as well as good food.

Trends, in general, show that:

- More chefs are women.
- Institutional foodservices make hospital, prison, and armed services food more appealing.
- Young and old are making fortunes on "specialty" foods.
- Restaurant schools are enlarging and streamlining their programs.
- Everybody's being catered to! People who don't have time to cook want to serve their friends "homemade" food made elsewhere.
- Fast food is breaking out of the burger-mold. Salad bars and yogurt ice cream are among the new trends. Teens are in greater demand than ever at these serve-a-meal-in-a-minute eateries. They're taking the place of older people, who are looking for better-paying jobs.

That is part of what's new. But let's start at the beginning: schooling. Earlier chapters gave you a thorough and still-valid rundown on schooling from junior high and high school vocational schools to the college-level restaurant schools. A brief review will highlight what is new and different in this area.

High schools continue to cater to students' interests. At the Upper Dublin High School in Fort Washington, Pennsylvania, teens are invited to enroll in Project Free Enterprise, a summer program of management internships at places like Burger King. Other innovative programs exist around the country.

Vo-tech schools had their culinary students prepare meals for a "famous chefs" convention. These high school students produced outstanding meals for such cooking luminaries as Craig Claiborne. Their efforts won them praise and in some cases, job offers.

By the time students graduate from high school they may have developed an interest in the restaurant business in one form or another. One way to pursue that interest is to elect a foodservice major at a college or university. A college diploma with a concentration in their field often earns a graduating student a slot in the managerial ranks of the restaurant business. (See Appendix A.)

The restaurant schools offer a total immersion route to culinary education. The country's many restaurant schools (see Chapter IX) continue to attract students interested in careers in the culinary world. The Restaurant School in Philadelphia has added a course that awards a degree a year earlier than more comprehensive programs. This addition to the already wide curriculum is an Associate Degree in Specialized Technology, enabling a student to go immediately into the foodservice industry as a trained professional.

The International Culinary Arts Institute in Baltimore has added a European campus where future hotel managers may train and those in other foodservice fields can develop a Continental touch. The Institute has also added an Innkeeping course to meet the growing popularity of the country inn and the "bed and breakfast."

For those who might like to attend a restaurant school far away but not *too* far away, there is Canada's Institut de Tourisme et d'Hôtellerie de Québec, the largest hotel and restaurant management school in the world. The bilingual school graduates students who are equipped to tackle any culinary job.

In one of the school's twenty-three laboratories, student bartenders, working with colored water instead of alcohol, learn to mix drinks. Elsewhere, teacher-chefs reveal the arts of great entrees, sauces, and pastries.

Whatever their field, students value the Institut's 70,000-recipe library and its videotapes on cooking techniques. If a student runs into trouble with a Béarnaise Sauce he need only run a tape to find out where he went wrong.

While restaurant education broadens its scope, a lot of action is visible in the many areas of the foodservice industry.

Fast-food management, for instance, is considering home delivery. (One pizza chain is experimenting with a delivery truck that bakes pizza en route to a customer's home.) Fast-food outlets still play a major role in the eating-out habits of Americans young and old, but they must keep up with the competition and the changes in food tastes. The most significant new trend is toward a more healthful, more slimming diet. Thus, places that once glorified the hamburger now promote large, wholesome salads as well.

But some things never change. A McDonald's workday is pretty much the same as described in Chapter II. Everyone from counter workers to director of operations enjoys the stability and up-beat spirit of working for this chain.

Dawn Martinez, store manager of the Horsham, Pennsylvania, McDonald's, is twenty-three. She left a career as legal secretary to return to McDonald's, where she had worked as a teenager. "I like the action," she says. And the staff likes Dawn. Horsham counter operators such as Samatha Dugan, nineteen, feel that Dawn is a sort of "big sister" to all of them. Dawn would like to go to McDonald's Hamburger U. in Chicago. Hamburger U. offers special training for those who like the food business. Completion of the intensive two-week course guarantees an entree into the upper echelons of any restaurant chain.

Fast food is only a part of the foodservice industry. Foodservice is also "institutional," or large-scale, cooking. Among these sectors are foodservice for the armed forces, the prisons, and the hospitals.

These careers were covered briefly in Chapter V, but they form a large part of the entire restaurant industry and across the nation employ tremendous numbers of food professionals.

One of the most exciting developments of institutional food-service is the superior quality of the meals and the individual touches that please those who are "customers" for long periods of time.

The U.S. Navy is one example. The aircraft carrier *Independence* is a floating city, and within this seabound city are 5,000 sailors needing to be fed "three squares" a day. The Navy's foodservice system in Washington, D.C., supplies all of the food and food personnel for this and other Navy ships.

Food becomes a matter of prime importance to the sailor at sea for months at a time. Commander E.J. Landerkin, head of food management on the *Independence*, realizes that. He and his team of officers and full-time sailor-cooks offer attractive and nutritious meals, with two salad bars. There is also a fast-food restaurant where sailors can enjoy the informal atmosphere and traditional fare of eateries back home. But dinner is still the highlight of the day. On a particular night they may help decimate the 660 pounds of a tasty dish brought on board for that one meal.

Food is also the high point of the day for prison inmates. Recently, the Pennsylvania Department of Corrections won the Silver Platter Award from the International Foodservice Manufacturers Association for excellence in food service. Perhaps that is because men like Keith Graham, chief of food services for the prison system, feel that prisoners deserve good, attractive food. Graham has also instituted diet programs and established an inmate cooking school. These prison students will have a useful culinary background when they return to the world.

When someone says institutional foodservice, hospitals often come to mind. Until recently, hospital food has had a bad reputation. Robert V. Vasek, director of food services at Rolling Hill Hospital in Elkins Park, Pennsylvania, is aware of that image. "A lot of people," says Vasek, "think hospital food is prepackaged or canned. It's not. It's prepared fresh every day." It's true that many U.S. hospitals are not able to make that claim, but the majority are working hard to change their reputation.

Rolling Hill Hospital has gone high-tech with its new computer system, which makes for efficient food preparation. In the cafeteria expertly prepared food is complemented by floral arrangements and attractive garnishes. "The extensive kitchen staff," says Vasek, "is trained to produce meals that make patients feel better. The medical staff enjoys nourishing food designed to see them through their twelve- to twenty-four-hour days."

What's new for the maitre d'? Primarily, he has become more

than just the person who manages dining-room seating. He or she may well be the dining-room manager, as well. The maitre d'/dining-room manager may hire and fire personnel, administer training programs, and see that food is served at the proper temperature.

Women are entering the elite field of maitre d'. Although they have long been responsible for table seating at modest restaurants, they are now breaking into the big time with their reorganized managerial and personnel skills.

"Big time," incidentally, can mean $100,000 a year in tips, salary, and bonuses if the maitre d' is shepherding the clients of America's finest eateries. In these first-class restaurants maitre d's act as culinary ambassadors. They know their customers, their tastes—even where they like to sit. In turn, they are financially rewarded for V.I.P. treatment.

But that is far in the future. A successful maitre d'/dining-room manager must wear many hats before he or she rules over a four-star restaurant, a private club, or an ocean liner dining salon. The progression is often from waiter to banquet assistant to banquet manager and then to maitre d'.

In a good restaurant, the dining-room manager and the chef are a team. That team today may be male/male, male/female, or even a total woman venture. As we saw in Chapter VI, women have made great strides in a field that had always been dominated by men, and they don't intend to lose their new status. In a women's Culinary Alliance, based in Los Angeles, women chefs "network" to share cooking experiences, both positive and negative. One thing they agree upon is the continuing need to prove themselves equal to their male counterparts. That means working harder and longer to achieve a distinctive reputation.

Whether male or female, today's chef is helped by the computer. More and more restaurants are using computer systems to link the dining room and kitchen. The result is that food orders are more accurate and are delivered more quickly.

Marilyn Anthony, Head Chef Instructor of Philadelphia's Restaurant School, has some interesting things to say about the direction of today's cuisine. "Although restaurant schools still emphasize the varied styles of cooking—sauce-laden, *nouveau* French or Cajun, for instance—there is now a reverse trend toward superior preparation of more basic foods. That means careful cooking of a steak, or preparing a vegetable to preserve its freshness and flavor."

Other culinary trends include greater emphasis on regional American dishes, the introduction of organic foods in elegant restaurants, and selective use of fresh herbs.

Chefs, maitre d's, restaurant managers, waiters and waitresses collectively make a restaurant's reputation. Chapter VIII, "Owning Your Own Restaurant," sounded the warnings about restaurant ownership. It's a risky business unless you're well endowed with money and smarts.

San Francisco, home to 2,600 restaurants, still experiences a high failure rate. In a 1989 survey the word in this gourmet-conscious city was that good food is only part of the recipe for a restaurant's success.

"You have to keep your name out front," explains John Riggio, owner of the bistro Café Riggio. And this restaurateur explains how to do it. Effective advertising, marketing, and public relations can turn a restaurant into a household word. Every PR method—including thank-you notes mailed to patrons—helps bring customers back.

Cut-throat competition is not a problem only in San Francisco. Metropolises like New York City or small, trendy towns like Doylestown, Pennsylvania, compete for customers, too. Entrepreneurs in these and other cities are getting into the restaurant act even though they're aware of the risks. In their efforts to stay afloat, restaurant owners often submit to eighteen-hour days, endure last-minute service crises, and fill in for missing staff members—whatever it takes to keep going.

John Riggio sums up the business in terms of extremes. "When things go wrong, I think about walking off the Golden Gate Bridge. But when all goes well, it's like a symphony. There's real creativity in having a restaurant and a tremendous gratification in it."

Rich Melman knows that feeling of reward. Rich is the owner of nearly thirty successful restaurants around the country. His chain is based on a sense of fun and makes good use of Melman's artistic sensibilities. "An artist uses canvases...restaurants are my canvas," says the director of Lettuce Entertain You Enterprises, Inc.

Rich started at the very bottom of the culinary ladder: he peddled ice cream and peanuts on the beaches of Lake Michigan. Later he managed his father's delicatessens. Under his management, the delis prospered, but when Melman asked to become a partner in the business, his father refused to take him on. Undaunted, Melman went on to put his own stamp on the restaurant industry.

The young entrepreneur's sense of humor led him to give his places names such as Café Ba-Ba-Reeba. His business sense helped him run them efficiently, yet he pays special attention to his customers' food interests.

This concern for menu appeal is all-important to Melman. When Rich planned to open a Mexican restaurant, for example, he visited the country to gather ideas to give his place authenticity. Such attention to detail results in bonanzas for him.

Even TV personality Oprah Winfrey is excited about Rich Melman, so much so that she has chosen him as a restaurant partner. Winfrey is calling her new enterprise The Eccentric. She feels that Melman creates "theater" with his restaurants and that as a coowner she is going on stage. If Geraldo Rivera, the controversial talk-show host, shows up, Miss Winfrey promises that he'll get "...fire-grilled chicken; we soak it in chilies first!"

Many restaurants have catering facilities. But, as mentioned in Chapter VII, catering as a business is assuredly a sign of the 1990s. Kids do it, single moms do it—even royalty does it! Marina Ogilvy, the daughter of Princess Alexandra (niece of the Queen of England), has just finished a one-year catering course. She should have little difficulty getting assignments from the Royal Family. What a credit for her résumé!

Many caterers—royal or not—are surprisingly young. Take Kenneth Carter of Gary, Indiana. Kenneth is fifteen years old, and his company, TC Catering Service, is grossing well over $10,000 a year. But Ken is *old* now—he started catering at thirteen.

Ken started his own business because no one would hire him. Food preparation appealed to him because he had always enjoyed cooking. He volunteered his services to a caterer to get some experience, and he realized that he could offer customers as bountifully laden platters as his boss at half the price. Soon Ken was into a full-time business with a staff of ten.

Ken Carter recently received a letter of congratulation from the Hutchinson Town Club, an organization of black chefs in Kentucky. When he finishes high school, he has his choice of two top spots for continuing his education. He has been accepted at the Culinary Institute of America in Hyde Park, New York, and Cornell University's School of Hotel Management. The question is not where he will go, but will the instructors teach *him*, or will he teach them?

New trends in catering are also newsworthy. In some cases they're downright ingenious. For instance, a recent Associated Press article highlighted a fitness trainer who became a caterer to struggling dieters. Yolanda Bergman did not plan to abandon her job at Jane Fonda's Workout Studios in New York. But she noticed that her clients' eating habits were offsetting the value of the workouts. At first she advised, but when that didn't get results she began to *buy* the right foods for her customers.

Now Yolanda has a staff of eight and delivers healthful foods seven days a week to determined dieters and health-conscious patrons.

News of such unusual catering ventures should not overshadow the growth of traditional catering. Catering is becoming more popular for civic celebrations, corporate affairs, bridal showers, and children's parties. As we become more of a service economy, there is a very definite niche for those who like to prepare food for others.

And now catering has a new dimension, an area of food distribution that has developed since this book was written. Fully prepared, high-quality take-home foods are available not far from home. Although many supermarkets are launching salad bars and take-out counters, the concept really got its start at gourmet food stores and the specialty food stands found in many farmer's markets.

Today's farmer's market has little in common with the earlier outlets for home-grown produce. The modern market with its trendy candy and gift booths is a magnet for shoppers. But the carefully prepared food at various booths is the market's greatest appeal.

"Don't have time to cook but still want that just-cooked aroma and taste?" ask Ruth and Elliot Rothman, owners of a food outlet in a suburban Philadelphia Farmer's Market. "Buffet Gourmet should be on your list of important places to shop."

This attractive husband-wife team merged their talents to create their extensive line of food offerings. Ruth's and Elliot's parents were both owners of food businesses. Growing up in that atmosphere helped prepare them for a business of their own—a catering business. They refined and expanded upon marvelous recipes and developed a clientele throughout the Philadelphia area. Now Buffet Gourmet is a logical extension of their talents.

The Rothmans explain their success. "Our food is an instant hit, whether it's prepared for the person who hasn't time to cook, who has a gourmet's palate, or both. We supply everything for a meal—salads, meats, and desserts. Our food has only to be warmed (or chilled), and a gourmet meal is ready in a flash." Since they're never content with yesterday's successes, the Rothmans are always searching for new and exciting foods to bring to their growing list of loyal customers.

Catering and ready-to-eat foods are among the fast-growing foodservice areas. In fact, the whole restaurant industry is destined to expand in the 1990s. As future contributors to its growth, you young people in school and college are entering a field with a solid future. Not only are there many different ways you can participate in the profession, but you can also bring your own ideas with you. Your creativity may take you to the very top. Not many career fields can claim that distinction.

Appendix **A**

Programs in Hotel, Restaurant, Institutional Management

The following listings are provided courtesy National Institute for the Foodservice Industry.

SENIOR COLLEGES

The foodservice industry encompasses hospitals, nursing homes, and other institutions that place a heavy emphasis on dietetics. Such programs that offer a foodservice management option are flagged with a "D". An "M" indicates postgraduate degrees.

ALABAMA

Auburn University
D Foodservice Administration
Department of Nutrition and Foods
Auburn, AL 36849

Tuskegee Institute
Foodservice Management
Department of Home Economics
Tuskegee, AL 36088

ALASKA

University of Alaska
Travel Industry Management Program
Department of Business Administration
Fairbanks, AK 99701

ARIZONA

Northern Arizona University
Lodging, Restaurant and Tourism Administration
Campus Box 15066
Flagstaff, AZ 86011

CALIFORNIA

California Polytechnic State University
D Dietetics/Food Administration
Home Economics Department
San Luis Obispo, CA 93407

California State University
D Food and Nutrition
Home Economics Department
Chico, CA 95929

California State University, Long Beach
D Foodservice Systems Administration
Department of Home Economics
1250 Bellflower Boulevard
Long Beach, CA 90840

California State Polytechnic University
Hotel, Restaurant and Travel Management Department
3801 West Temple Avenue
Pomona, CA 91768

Golden Gate University
M Hotel, Restaurant and Institutional Management
536 Mission Street
San Francisco, CA 94133

Loma Linda University
D Nutrition and Dietetics
11234 Anderson
Loma Linda, CA 92350

United States International Unviersity
Hotel and Restaurant Management
10455 Pomerado Road
San Diego, CA 92131

University of California, Berkeley
D Nutrition and Clinical Dietetics
127 Morgan Hall
Berkeley, CA 94720

University of California, Davis
D Dietetics-Food Service Management

Department of Nutrition
Davis, CA 95616

University of San Francisco
Hospitality Management
2130 Fulton Street
San Francisco, CA 94117

COLORADO

Colorado State University
Restaurant Mangement
Department of Food Science and Nutrition
Gifford Building
Fort Collins, CO 80523

Metropolitan State College
Hospitality, Meeting, Travel Administration
1006 11th Street, Box 60
Denver, CO 80204

University of Denver
M School of Hotel and Restaurant Management
2030 East Evans
Denver, CO 80208

CONNECTICUT

University of New Haven
M Hotel, Restaurant Management, Dietetics and Tourism Administration
300 Orange Avenue
West Haven, CT 06516

DELAWARE

Widener University
Hotel and Restaurant Management
P.O. Box 713 Concord Pike
Wilmington, DE 19803

FLORIDA

Bethune-Cookman College
Hospitality Management Administration
Division of Business
640 Second Avenue
Daytona Beach, FL 32015

Biscayne College
Tourism, Hospitality Management and International Enterprise
16400 NW 32nd Avenue
Miami, FL 33054

Florida International University
M School of Hospitality Management
Tamiami Trail
Miami, FL 33199

Florida State University
Department of Hotel and Restaurant Administration
College of Business
Tallahassee, FL 32306

Webber College
Hospitality Management Department
Route 27-A
Babson Park, FL 33827

GEORGIA

Georgia State University
Department of Hotel, Restaurant and Travel Administration
University Plaza
Atlanta, GA 30303

Morris Brown College
Hotel Management Department
643 Martin Luther King, Jr. Drive
Atlanta, GA 30314

University of Georgia
D Food Service Management
Dawson Hall
Athens, GA 30602

HAWAII

Brigham Young University
Travel, Hotel, and Restaurant Management
55–220 Kulanui Street
Laie, HI 96762

University of Hawaii
School of Travel Industry Management
2404 Maile Way, A 303
Honolulu, HI 96822

ILLINOIS
Bradley University
D Foods, Dietetics and Nutrition
Home Economics Department
Peoria, IL 61625

Eastern Illinois University
D Dietetics
School of Home Economics
Charleston, IL 61920

Northern Illinois University
D Coordinated Undergraduate Program in Dietetics
Department of Home Economics
DeKalb, IL 60115

Rosary College
D Foods and Nutrition
7900 West Division Street
River Forest, IL 60305

Southern Illinois University
Foods and Nutrition
Carbondale, IL 62901

University of Illinois
M Restaurant Management
274 Bevier Hall
Urbana, IL 61801

Western Illinois University
Foods and Lodging Management
Home Economics Department
Macomb, IL 61455

INDIANA
Purdue University
M Department of Restaurant, Hotel and Institutional Management
Stone Hall
West Lafayette, IN 47907

IOWA
Iowa State University
M Hotel, Restaurant and Institution Management
11 MacKay Hall
Ames, IA 50011

KANSAS

Kansas State University
Restaurant Management
105 Justin Hall
Manhattan, KS 66506

KENTUCKY

Morehead State University
D Food Service Administration
Home Economics Department
UPO 889, MSU
Morehead KY 40351

Transylvania University
Hotel, Restaurant, Tourism Administration
300 North Broadway
Lexington, KY 40508

University of Kentucky
Restaurant Management
Nutrition and Food Science Department
205 Erickson Hall
Lexington, KY 40506

Western Kentucky University
Institution Administration
Department of Home Economics
Bowling Green, KY 42101

LOUISIANA

University of New Orleans
School of Hotel, Restaurant and Tourism Administration
New Orleans, LA 70148

MARYLAND

University of Maryland
M D Institution Administration
Department of Food, Nutrition and Institution Administration
College Park, MD 20742

University of Maryland-Eastern Shore
Department of Hotel and Restaurant Management
P.O. Box 1001
Princess Anne, MD 21853

MASSACHUSETTS

Boston University—Metropolitan College

Hotel and Food Administration
755 Commonwealth Avenue, Room B-3
Boston, MA 02215

University of Massachusetts
M Department of Hotel, Restaurant and Travel Administration
101 Flint Laboratory
Amherst, MA 01003

MICHIGAN

Central Michigan University
Hospitality Services Administration
108 North Hall
Mt. Pleasant, MI 48859

Eastern Michigan University
D Coordinated Undergraduate Program in Dietetics
202 Roosevelt Hall
Ypsilanti, MI 48197

Ferris State College
Hospitality Management
South Commons
Big Rapids, MI 49307

Grand Valley State Colleges
Hospitality and Tourism Management
Allendale, MI 49401

Mercy College of Detroit
Foodservice Management
8200 W. Outer Drive
Detroit, MI 48219

Michigan State University
M School of Hotel, Restaurant and Institutional Management
425 Eppley Center
East Lansing, MI 48824

Siena Heights College
Hotel, Restaurant and Institutional Management
1247 East Siena Heights Drive
Adrian, MI 49221

MINNESOTA

Mankato State University
D Food and Nutrition
Home Economics Department
MSU Box 44
Mankato, MN 56001

Southwest State University
Hotel, Restaurant and Institutional Management
Marshall, MN 56258

MISSISSIPPI

University of Southern Mississippi
Hotel and Restaurant Administration
Southern Station Box 10025
Hattiesburg, MS 39401

MISSOURI

Central Missouri State University
Hotel, Motel Restaurant Administration
250 Grinstead Hall
Warrensburg, MO 64093

University of Missouri
Food Service and Lodging Management
223 Gentry Hall
Columbia, MO 65211

NEBRASKA

University of Nebraska
Food Service Management
60th and Dodge
Omaha, NE 68182

NEVADA

University of Nevada, Las Vegas
M College of Hotel Administration
4505 Maryland Parkway
Las Vegas, NE 89154

NEW HAMPSHIRE

New Hampshire College
Hotel and Restaurant Management
2500 North River Road
Manchester, NH 03104

University of New Hampshire
Hotel Administration Program
McConnell Hall
Durham, NH 03824

NEW JERSEY

Fairleigh Dickinson University
M Hotel & Restaurant Management
College of Business
Rutherford, NJ 07070

Montclair State College
D Food Service Management
Normal Avenue
Upper Montclair, NJ 07043

NEW YORK

Cornell University
M School of Hotel Administration
Statler Hall
Ithaca, NY 14853

Marymount College
D Food and Nutrition
Department of Home Economics
Marymount Avenue
Tarrytown, NY 10591

New York Institute of Technology
Hotel/Restaurant Administration
207 Simonson House
Old Westbury, NY 11568

New York University
M Foodservice Management
239 Greene Street, 537 East Building
New York, NY 10003

Niagara University
Hospitality Management
Institute of Transportation, Travel and Tourism
Niagara, NY 14109

Pratt Institute
D Department of Food Science and Management
215 Ryerson Street, Room 318, DeKalb Hall
Brooklyn NY 11205

Rochester Institute of Technology
Department of Food, Hotel and Tourism Management
One Lomb Memorial Drive
Rochester, NY 14623

State University College at Buffalo
Food Systems Management

Nutrition and Food Science Department
1300 Elmwood Avenue
Buffalo, NY 14222

State University of New York, Oneonta
Food and Business
Department of Home Economics
Oneonta, NY 13820

Syracuse University
D Dietetics Management
Department of Human Nutrition
301 Slocum Hall
Syracuse, NY 13210

NORTH CAROLINA

Appalachian State University
Food Systems Management
Department of Home Economics
Boone, NC 28608

Barber-Scotia College
Hotel, Restaurant Management
School of Arts, Science and Business
145 Cabarrus Avenue West
Concord, NC 28025

East Carolina University
D Food, Nutrition and Institution Management
School of Home Economics
Greenville, NC 27834

North Carolina Central University
D Institutional Management
Department of Home Economics
P.O. Box 19615
Durham, NC 27707

University of North Carolina, Greensboro
D Food, Nutrition, Food Service Management
School of Home Economics
Greensboro, NC 27412

NORTH DAKOTA

North Dakota State University
Hotel, Motel, Restaurant Management
Food and Nutrition Department
Fargo, ND 58105

OHIO

Ashland College
Hotel/Restaurant Management
College Avenue
Ashland, OH 44805

Miami University
D Food Management, Home Economics
260 McGuffey Hall
Oxford, OH 45056

The Ohio State University
Restaurant Management Program
1787 Neil Avenue
Columbus, OH 43210

OKLAHOMA

Oklahoma State University
Hotel and Restaurant Administration
HEW 419
Stillwater, OK 74078

OREGON

Oregon State University
Hotel and Restaurant Management Program
Corvallis, OR 97331

PENNSYLVANIA

Drexel University
Food Service Systems Management
34th and Market Streets
Building 13
Philadelphia, PA 19104

East Stroudsburg University
Department of Hotel and Resort Management
Prospect Street
East Stroudsburg, PA 18301

Indiana University of Pennsylvania
Department of Food and Nutrition
10 Ackerman Hall
Indiana, PA 15705

Mansfield State College
D Food Service/Dietetics

Home Economics Building
Mansfield, PA 16933

Mercyhurst College
Hotel and Restaurant Management
Glenwood Hills
Erie, PA 16546

The Pennsylvania State University
Hotel, Restaurant and Institution Management
20 Henderson Human Development
University Park, PA 16802

RHODE ISLAND

Bryant College
Department of Hotel Restaurant and Institutional Management
Smithfield, RI 02917

Johnson and Wales College
Hospitality Management
8 Abbott Park Place
Providence, RI 02903

SOUTH CAROLINA

University of South Carolina
Hotel, Restaurant and Tourism Administration
084 Coliseum, District A-1
Columbia, SC 29208

SOUTH DAKOTA

Black Hills State College
Travel Industry Management
1200 University
Spearfish, SD 57783

South Dakota State University
Nutrition and Food Science Department
College of Home Economics
P.O. Box 2275A, SDSU
Brookings, SD 57007

TENNESSEE

Belmont College
School of Hospitality Business
Belmont Boulevard.
Nashville, TN 37203

University of Tennessee
M Tourism, Food and Lodging Administration
College of Home Economics
Knoxville, TN 37916

TEXAS

Huston-Tillotson College
Hospitality Management
1820 East 8th Street
Austin, TX 78702

Texas Tech University
Restaurant, Hotel and Institutional Management
Box 4170, TTU
Lubbock, TX 79409

Texas Woman's University
D Coordinated Undergraduate Program in Dietetics
P.O. Box 24134, TWU Station
Denton, TX 76204

University of Houston
Hilton Hotel and Restaurant Management College
4800 Calhoun Drive
Houston, TX 77004

UTAH

Brigham Young University
M Food Systems Administration
2218 SFLC
Provo, UT 84602

VIRGINIA

James Madison University
Hotel and Restaurant Management Program
Harrisonburg, VA 22807

Radford University
Food Service Management
P.O. Box 5797
Radford, VA 24141

Virginia Polytechnic Institute and State University
M Hotel, Restaurant and Institutional Management
322 Wallace Hall
Blacksburg, VA 24061

Virginia State University
Hotel Restaurant Management
Box 427, VSU
Petersburg, VA 23803

WASHINGTON
Washington State University
Hotel and Restaurant Administration
245 Todd Hall
Pullman, WA 99164

Washington State University
Hotel and Restaurant Administration
1108 East Columbia
Seattle, WA 98122

WEST VIRGINIA
Shepherd College
Hotel/Motel and Restaurant Management
Shepherdstown, WV 25443

WISCONSIN
University of Wisconsin-Madison
D Foodservice Administration
Babcock Hall, 1605 Linden Drive
Madison, WI 53706

University of Wisconsin-Stout
Hotel and Restaurant Management
Home Economics Building
Menomonie, WI 54751

JUNIOR COMMUNITY COLLEGES AND CULINARY SCHOOLS

ALABAMA
Community College of the Air Force
Restaurant Management
CCAF/AYL Building 836
Maxwell AFB, AL 36112

Bessemer State Technical College
Food Service

P.O. Box 308
Bessemer, AL 35021

Carver State Technical College
Food Preparation and Services
414 Stanton Street
Mobile, AL 36617

Jefferson State Junior College
Food Service Management and Technology
2601 Carson Road
Birmingham, AL 35215

Lawson State Community college
Commercial Food Preparation
3060 Wilson Road SW
Birmingham, AL 35221

Wallace State Community College
Quantity Foods and Nutrition
P.O. Box 250
Hanceville, AL 35077

ALASKA

Anchorage Community College
Food Service Technology
2533 Providence Avenue
Anchorage, AK 99504

ARIZONA

Pima Community College
Hospitality Education Program
P.O. Box 5027
Tucson, AZ 85703

Phoenix College
Foodservice Administration
1202 West Thomas Road
Phoenix, AZ 85013

Scottsdale Community College
Hospitality Program
9000 East Chaparral Road
Scottsdale, AZ 85253

ARKANSAS

Quapaw Vocational Technical
Food Service Management

201 Vo-Tech Drive
Hot Springs, AR 71913
Southern Arkansas University-Technical Branch
Hotel and Restaurant Management
P.O. Box 3048
Camden, AR 71701

CALIFORNIA
American River College
Food Service Management
4700 College Oak Drive
Sacramento, CA 95841

Bakersfield College
Hotel, Restaurant and Institutional Management
1801 Panorama Drive
Bakersfield, CA 93305

California Culinary Academy
Professional Chef Program
215 Fremont Street
San Francisco, CA 94105

Cañada College
Hotel, Restaurant and Institution Management
4200 Farm Hill Boulevard
Redwood City, CA 94061

Chaffey Community College
Food Service Management Training
5885 Haven
Alta Loma, CA 91701

Columbia College
Hospitality Management
P.O. Box 1849
Columbia, CA 95310

Contra Costa College
Culinary Arts
2600 Mission Bell Drive
San Pablo, CA 94806

Cypress College
Culinary Arts Department
9200 Valley View Boulevard
Cypress, CA 90630

College of the Desert
School of Culinary Arts

43500 Monterey Avenue
Palm Desert, CA 92260

Diablo Valley College
Hotel and Restaurant Management Program
321 Golf Club Road
Pleasant Hill, CA 94523

El Camino College
Food Service Management
16007 Crenshaw Boulevard
Torrance, CA 90506

Glendale Community College
Food Service and Management Program
1500 North Verdugo Road
Glendale, CA 91208

Grossmont College
Food Service Management
8800 Grossmont College Drive
El Cajon, CA 92020

Lake Tahoe Community College
Innkeeping and Restaurant Operations
P.O. Box 14445
South Lake Tahoe, CA 95602

Laney Community College
Food Preparation and Service
900 Fallon Street
Oakland, CA 94607

Los Angeles City College
Family and Consumer Studies
855 North Vermont Avenue
Los Angeles, CA 90029

Los Angeles Trade-Technical College
Hotel-Motel Management/Culinary Arts
400 West Washington Boulevard
Los Angeles, CA 90015

Merced College
Home Economics
3600 M Street
Merced, CA 95340

Modesto Junior College
Food Service
West Campus—Blue Gum Avenue
Modesto, CA 95350

Orange Coast College
Food Service and Hotel Management
2701 Fairview Road
Costa Mesa, CA 92626

Oxnard College
Hotel and Restaurant Management
4000 South Rose Avenue
Oxnard, CA 93033

Pasadena City College
Food Service Instruction
1570 East Colorado Boulevard
Pasadena, CA 91106

Saddleback College
Hospitality Management
5500 Irvine Center Drive
Irvine, CA 92714

San Diego Community College District
Food Services/Hotel, Motel Management
3375 Camino Del Rio South
San Diego, CA 92108

San Diego Mesa College
Hotel, Motel Management
7250 Mesa College Drive
San Diego, CA 92111

City College of San Francisco
Hotel and Restaurant Department
50 Phelan Avenue
San Franscisco, CA 94112

San Joaquin Delta Community College
Food Service Industry
5151 Pacific Avenue
Stockton, CA 95207

Santa Barbara City College
Hotel and Restaurant Management
721 Cliff Drive
Santa Barbara, CA 93109

Shasta College
Foodservice and Culinary Arts
1065 North Old Oregon Trail
Redding, CA 96099

Ventura College
Food Management

4667 Telegraph Road
Ventura, CA 93003

West Valley College
Food Service Restaurant Management
14000 Fruitvale Avenue
Saratoga, CA 95070

Yuba Community College
Food Service Management
2088 North Beale Road
Marysville, CA 95901

COLORADO

Community College of the Air Force
Restaurant Management/Management-Logistics Department
3440th Technical Training Group
Lowry AFB, CO 80230

Aurora Public School Technical Center
Food Management Training
500 Buckley Road
Aurora, CO 80011

Colorado Mountain College/Timberline Campus
Ski/Resort Management
Leadville, CO 80461

Front Range Community College
Dietetic Technology
3645 West 12th Avenue
Westminster, CO 80030

Emily Griffith Opportunity School
Denver Public School System
Foodservice Production and Management
1250 Welton Street
Denver, CO 80204

Pikes Peak Community College
Food Management Program
5675 South Academy Boulevard
Colorado Springs, CO 80906

CONNECTICUT

Manchester Community College
Hotel and Foodservice Management Program
60 Bidwell Street
Manchester, CT 06040

Mattatuck Community College
Culinary Arts
750 Chase Parkway
Waterbury, CT 06708

University of New Haven
Hotel/Restaurant Management
300 Orange Avenue
West Haven, CT 06516

South Central Community College
Dietetic Technician/Nutrition Care
60 Sargent Drive
New Haven, CT 06511

DELAWARE

Delaware Technical Community College
Hospitality Management
P.O. Box 610
Georgetown, DE 19947

Widener University
Hotel and Restaurant Management
P.O. Box 7139-Concord Pike
Wilmington, DE 19803

FLORIDA

Atlantic Vocational Technical Center
Culinary Arts
4700 NW Coconut Creek Parkway
Coconut Creek, FL 33066

Broward Community College
Restaurant Management; Hotel-Motel Administration
3501 SW Davie Road
Fort Lauderdale, FL 33314

Daytona Beach Community College
Hospitality Management
P.O. Box 1111
Daytona Beach, FL 32015

Florida Junior College at Jacksonville
Hospitality Management
3939 Roosevelt Boulevard
Jacksonville, FL 32205

Gulf Coast Community College
Hotel/Motel, Restaurant Management

5230 West Highway 98
Panama City, FL 32401

Hillsborough Community College
Hotel and Restaurant Management
P.O. Box 22127
Tampa, FL 33622

Manatee Junior College
Food Service-Restaurant, Hotel-Motel Management
5840 26th Street, West
Bradenton, FL 33507

Miami-Dade Community College
Hotel, Restaurant and Institutional Management
300 NE 2nd Avenue
Miami, FL 33132

Mid-Florida Technical Institute
Hospitality Program
2900 West Oakridge Road
Orlando, FL 32809

North Technical Education Center
Culinary Arts
7071 Garden Road
Riviera Beach, FL 33404

Okaloosa-Walton Junior College
Commercial Foods-Industrial Education
100 College Boulevard
Niceville, FL 32578

Palm Beach Junior College
Hospitality Management Program
4200 South Congress Avenue
Lake Worth, FL 33461

College of the Palm Beaches
Hotel-Motel Management
660 Fern Street
West Palm Beach, FL 33401

Pensacola Junior College
Dietetic Technician/Hotel and Restaurant Management
1000 College Boulevard
Pensacola, FL 32504

Pinellas Vocational Technical Institute
Culinary Arts Department
6100 154th Avenue, North
Clearwater, FL 33540

Sarasota County Vocational Technical Center
Culinary Arts/Hospitality Management
4748 Beneva Road
Sarasota, FL 33583

Seminole Community College
Food Service/Culinary Arts
Hwy. 17–92
Sanford, FL 32771

St. Augustine Technical Center
Commercial Foods/Culinary Arts Program
Collins Avenue at Del Monte Drive
St. Augustine, FL 32084

St. Petersburg Junior College
Hospitality Management
P.O. Box 13489
St. Petersburg, FL 33733

Valencia Community College
Hotel, Motel and Restaurant Management Training
P.O. Box 3028
Orlando, FL 32802

Webber College
Hospitality Management
Route 27-A
Babson Park, FL 33827

GEORGIA

Ben Hill-Irwin Area Vocational Technical School
Food Service
P.O. Box 1069
Fitzgerald, GA 31750

Georgia State University
Hotel, Restaurant and Travel Administration
University Plaza
Atlanta, GA 30303

Houston Vocational Center
Food Service Department
1311 Corder Road
Warner Robins, GA 31056

Macon Area Vocational Technical School
Quantity Food Service
3300 Macon Tech Drive
Macon, GA 31206

HAWAII

Cannon's International Business College of Honolulu
Hotel Front Office Procedures, Hotel Management
33 South King Street
Honolulu, HI 96813

Hawaii Community College
Food Service Department
1175 Manono Street
Hilo, HI 96720

Honolulu Community College
Commercial Baking
874 Dillingham Boulevard
Honolulu, HI 96817

Kapiolani Community College
Food Service and Hospitality Education
620 Pensacola Street
Honolulu, HI 96814

Leeward Community College
Food Service Program, Vocational Technical Division
96–045 Ala Ike
Pearl City, HI 96782

Maui Community College
Food Service Program
310 Kaahumanu Avenue
Kahului, HI 96732

Brigham Young University—Hawaii
Travel, Hotel, and Restaurant Management
55–220 Julanui Street
Laie, HI 96762

IDAHO

Boise State University
Food Service Technology
1910 University Drive
Boise, ID 83725

ILLINOIS

Chicago Hospitality Institute
Chicago City-Wide College
Foodservice and Hotel-Motel Management
30 East Lake Street
Chicago, IL 60601

College of DuPage
Foodservice Administration/Hotel-Motel Management
22nd Street and Lambert Road
Glen Ellyn, IL 60137

Elgin Community College
Hospitality Management
1700 Spartan Drive
Elgin, IL 60120

William Rainey Harper College
Food Service Management, Cooking and Baking
Algonquin and Roselle Roads
Palatine, IL 60067

Joliet Junior College
Culinary Arts/Hotel-Restaurant Management
1216 Houbolt Avenue
Joliet, IL 60436

Kennedy-King College
Food Management
6800 South Wentworth Avenue
Chicago, IL 60621

Lexington Institute
Foodservice and Lodging Program
10840 South Western Avenue
Chicago, IL 60643

Lincoln Trail College
Restaurant Management/Culinary Arts
RR 3
Robinson, IL 62454

Oakton Community College
Hotel-Motel Management Program
1600 East Golf Road
Des Plaines, IL 60016

Parkland College
Food Service Management
2400 West Bradley
Champaign, IL 61821

Sauk Valley College
Public Services-Food Services
Rural Route #5
Dixon, IL 61021

Southeastern Illinois College
Food Service Technology

Rural Route #4
Harrisburg, IL 62946

Triton College
Hospitality Industry Amdinistration
2000 Fifth Avenue
River Grove, IL 60171

Washburne Trade School
Chef Training
3233 West 31st Street
Chicago, IL 60623

John Wood Community College
Occupational Education
1919 North 18th Street
Quincy, IL 62301

INDIANA

**Indiana University—
Purdue University at Indianapolis**
Restaurant, Hotel, and Institutional Management
799 West Michigan Street
Indianapolis, IN 46241

Ivy Tech
Hospitality Careers
1315 East Washington Street
Indianapolis, IN 46202

Purdue University
Restaurant, Hotel and Institutional Management
Stone Hall
West Lafayette, IN 47907

Vincennes University
Restaurant and Foodservice Management
1st Street
Vincennes, IN 47591

IOWA

Des Moines Area Community College
Hospitality Careers
2006 Ankeny Boulevard
Ankeny, IA 50021

Indian Hills Community College
Chef Training, Bakery Training

Grandview and Elm
Ottumwa, IA 52501

Iowa Lakes Community College
Hotel/Motel and Restaurant Management
3200 College Drive
Emmetsburg, IA 50536

Iowa Western Community College
Food Service Management; Cooking and Baking
2700 College Road
Council Bluffs, IA 51501

Kirkwood Community College
Food Service Management
6301 Kirkwood Boulevard SW
Cedar Rapids, IA 52406

KANSAS

Butler County Community College
Food Service and Management
Towanda Avenue and Haverhill Road
El Dorado, KS 67042

Central College
Food Service/Home Economics
1200 South Main
McPherson, KS 67460

Johnson County Community College
Hospitality Management Program
12345 College at Quivira
Overland Park, KS 66210

Manhattan Area Vocational Technical School
Foodservice and Management
3136 Dickens Avenue
Manhattan, KS 66502

Northeast Kansas Area Vocational Technical School
Commercial Food Preparation/Restaurant Management
1501 West Riley
Atchison, KS 66002

Southwest Kansas Area Vocational Technical School
Foodservice Program
2nd and Comanche Streets
Dodge City, KS 67801

Wichita Area Vocational Technical School
Food Service Mid-Management and Culinary Arts

324 North Emporia
Wichita, KS 67202

KENTUCKY

Daviess County State Vocational Technical School
Commercial Foods
1901 SE Parkway
Owensboro, KY 42301

Elizabethtown State Vocational Technical School
Commercial Foods
505 University Drive
Elizabethtown, KY 42701

Jefferson Community College
Culinary Arts
109 East Broadway
Louisville, KY 40202

Northern Kentucky State Vocational Technical School
Commercial Foods Program
Amsterdam Road
Covington, KY 41011

West Kentucky State Vocational Technical School
Commercial Foods
Blandville Road, P.O. Box 7408
Paducah, KY 42001

LOUISIANA

Baton Rouge Vocational Technical Institute
Culinary Arts
3250 North Acadian Throughway
Baton Rouge, LA 70805

Sidney N. Collier Vocational Technical Institute
Culinary Arts
3727 Louisa Street
New Orleans, LA 70126

New Orleans Regional Vocational Technical Institute
Chef Apprenticeship
980 Navarre Avenue
New Orleans, LA 70124

Nicholls State University
Food Service Management
P.O. Box 2014 NSU
Thibodaux, LA 70301

MAINE

Eastern Maine Vocational Technical Institute
Food Technology
354 Hogan Road
Bangor, ME 04401

Southern Maine Vocational Technical Institute
Culinary Arts/Hotel, Motel and Restaurant Management
2 Fort Road
South Portland, ME 04106

MARYLAND

Baltimore's International Culinary Arts Institute
Restaurant Skills, Baking and Pastry Skills
19 South Gay Street
Baltimore, MD 21202

Essex Community College
Hotel-Motel and Restaurant-Club Management
7201 Rossville Boulevard
Baltimore, MD 21237

Hagerstown Junior College
Hospitality Program
751 Robinwood Drive
Hagerstown, MD 21740

Montgomery College
Hospitality Management
51 Mannakee Street
Rockville, MD 20850

Wor-Wic Tech Community College
Hotel, Motel and Restaurant Management
Route #3, Box 79
Berlin, MD 21811

MASSACHUSETTS

Berkshire Community College
Hotel and Restaurant Management
West Street
Pittsfield, MA 01201

Bunker Hill Community College
Hotel/Restaurant Management/Culinary Arts
New Rutherford Avenue
Charlestown, MA 02129

Cape Cod Community College
Hotel/Restaurant Management Program
Route 132
West Barnstable, MA 02668

Chamberlayne Junior College
Hotel and Institutional Management
128 Commonwealth Avenue
Boston, MA 02116

Endicott College
Hotel-Restaurant Management
376 Hale Street
Beverly, MA 01915

Holyoke Community College
Hospitality Management Program
303 Homestead Avenue
Holyoke, MA 01040

Laboure Junior College
Division of Dietetic Technology
2120 Dorchester Avenue
Boston, MA 02124

Newbury Junior College
Culinary Arts Program
129 Fisher Avenue
Brookline, MA 02146

Northeastern University
Hotel and Restaurant Management
102 Churchill Hall
Boston, MA 02115

Henry O. Peabody School
Culinary Arts
Nichols Street and Peabody Road
Norwood, MA 02062

Quincy Junior College
Hotel/Restaurant Management
34 Coddington Street
Quincy, MA 02169

MICHIGAN

The Career Development Center
Culinary Arts
5961 14th Street
Detroit, MI 48217

Davenport College of Business
Hospitality Management
415 East Fulton Street
Grand Rapids, MI 49503

Ferris State College
Food Service/Hospitality Management
South Commons
Big Rapids, MI 49307

Henry Ford Community College
Culinary Arts/Hotel Restaurant Management
5101 Evergreen Road
Dearborn, MI 48128

Gogebic Community College
Food Service
Jackson and Greenbush
Ironwood, MI 49938

Grand Rapids Junior College
Hotel/Restaurant Management; Culinary Arts
143 Bostwick NE
Grand Rapids, MI 49503

Lake Michigan College
Food Service Management
2755 East Napier Avenue
Benton Harbor, MI 49022

Lansing Community College
Food Service and Hotel/Motel Management
419 North Capitol Avenue
Lansing, MI 48901

Macomb Community College
Professional Foodservice
44575 Garfield Road
Mount Clemens, MI 48044

Charles S. Mott Community College
Food Management
1401 East Court Street
Flint, MI 48502

Northwestern Michigan College
Food Services Technology
1701 East Front Street
Traverse City, MI 49684

Northwood Institute-Michigan
Hotel/Restaurant Operation

3225 Cook Road
Midland, MI 48640

Oakland Community College
Hospitality Department
27055 Orchard Lake Road
Farmington Hills, MI 48018

Schoolcraft Community College
Culinary Arts
18600 Haggerty Road
Livonia, MI 48152

Siena Heights College
Hotel, Restaurant, and Institutional Management
1247 East Siena Heights Drive
Adrian, MI 49221

St. Clair County Community College
Foodservice Management/Vocational
323 Erie Street
Port Huron, MI 48060

State Technical Institute
Food Service Training
Alber Drive
Plainwell, MI 49080

Washtenaw Community College
Foods and Hospitality
4800 East Huron River Drive
Ann Arbor, MI 48106

Wayne County Community College
Culinary Arts Program
8551 Greenfield
Detroit, MI 48228

West Shore Community College
Hospitality Management
3000 North Stiles Road
Scottville, MI 49454

MINNESOTA

Alexandria Area Vocational Technical Institute
Hotel, Motel and Restaurant Management
1601 Jefferson Street
Alexandria, MN 56308

Canby Area Vocational Technical Institute
Food Service Management

1011 First Street West
Canby, MN 56220

Dakota County Area Vocational Technical Institute
Food Service and Chef Management
1300 145th Street East
Rosemount, MN 55068

Detroit Lakes Area Vocational Technical Institute
Commercial Cooking and Baking
Highway 34 East
Detroit Lakes, MN 56501

Duluth Area Vocational Technical Institute
Food Service Management
2101 Trinity Road
Duluth, MN 55811

Hennepin Technical Centers
Cook/Chef
1820 North Xenium Lane
Minneapolis, MN 55441

Mankato Area Vocational Technical Institute
Cook/Chef
1920 Lee Boulevard
North Mankato, MN 56001

University of Minnesota Technical College-Crookston
Hotel, Restaurant and Institutional Management
Highway 2 and 75, North
Crookston, MN 56716

Moorhead Area Vocational Technical Institute
Chef Training
1900 28th Avenue South
Moorhead, MN 56560

Normandale Community College
Hospitality Management Program
9700 France Avenue South
Bloomington, MN 55431

Willmar Area Vocational Technical Institute
Chefs Training and Food Service Management
Box 1097
Willmar, MN 56201

916 Vocational Technical Institute
Chef Training
3300 Century Avenue North
White Bear Lake, MN 55110

MISSISSIPPI

Hinds Junior College
Hotel, Motel and Restaurant Management
3925 Sunset Drive
Jackson, MS 39213

Meridian Junior College
Hotel and Restaurant Management
5500 Highway 19 North
Meridian, MS 39305

**Mississippi Gulf Coast Junior College—
  Jefferson Davis Campus**
Hotel, Motel and Restaurant Program
Handsboro Station
Gulfport, MS 39501

The Northeast Mississippi Junior College
Hotel, Motel and Restaurant Management
Booneville, MS 38829

MISSOURI

Crowder College
Hotel, Motel and Restaurant Program
Neosho, MO 64850

Jefferson College
Hotel/Restaurant Management
Hillsboro, MO 63050

Penn Valley Community College
Lodging and Food Service Management
3201 Southwest Trafficway
Kansas City, MO 64111

St. Louis Community College at Florissant Valley
Dietetic Technology
3400 Pershall Road
St. Louis, MO 63135

St. Louis Community College at Forest Park
Hospitality Restaurant Management Department
5600 Oakland Avenue
St. Louis, MO 63110

State Fair Community College
Food Service Management
1900 Clarendon Road
Sedalia, MO 65301

Three Rivers Community College
Hospitality Management Program
Three Rivers Boulevard
Poplar Bluff, MO 63901

MONTANA

Missoula Vocational Technical Center
Food Service
909 South Avenue West
Missoula, MT 59803

Western Montana College
Institutions and Resort Management
710 South Atlantic
Dillon, MT 59725

NEBRASKA

Central Community College
Hotel and Restaurant Management
P.O. Box 1024
Hastings, NE 68901

Metropolitan Technical Community College
Culinary Arts
P.O. Box 3777
Omaha, NE 68103

Southeast Community College-Lincoln Campus
Food Service Management
8800 "O" Street
Lincoln, NE 68520

NEVADA

Truckee Meadows Community College
Food Service Technology-Trade and Industry Division
7000 Dandini Boulevard
Sparks, NV 89512

NEW HAMPSHIRE

New Hampshire Vocational Technical College
Culinary Arts
2020 Riverside Drive
Berlin, NH 03570

University of New Hampshire
Thompson School of Applied Sciences

Food Service Management/Culinary Arts
Durham, NH 03824

NEW JERSEY

Academy of Culinary Arts
Atlantic Community College
Black Horse Pike
Mays Landing, NJ 08330

Atlantic Community College
Hospitality Management Program
Mays Landing, NJ 08330

Bergen Community College
Hotel/Restaurant Management Program
400 Paramus Road
Paramus, NJ 07652

Brookdale Community College
Food Service Management
Newman Springs Road
Lincroft, NJ 07738

Burlington County College
Hospitality Management
Pemberton-Browns Mill Road
Pemberton, NJ 08068

Camden County College
Dietetic Technician-Food Management
Box 200 B
Blackwood, NJ 08021

Career Center
Cape May County Vocational Technical School
Food Occupations
Cresthaven Road
Cape May Court House, NJ 08210

Hudson County Community College
Culinary Arts
161 Newkirk Street
Jersey City, NJ 07306

Middlesex County College
Hotel, Restaurant and Institution Management Department
10 Mill Road
Edison, NJ 08818

Ocean County College
Food Service Management
Toms River, NJ 08753

Salem County Vocational Technical Schools
Culinary Arts
R.D. #2, Box 350
Woodstown, NJ 08098

NEW MEXICO
Albuquerque Technical Vocational Institute
Culinary Arts
525 Buena Vista SE
Albuquerque, NM 87106

NEW YORK
Adirondack Community College
Commercial Cooking/Occupational Education
Bay Road
Glens Falls, NY 12801

The Culinary Institute of America
Culinary Arts
P.O. Box 53
Hyde Park, NY 12538

Erie Community College
Food Service Administration
Main and Youngs Road
Buffalo, NY 14221

Fulton-Montgomery Community College
Food Service Administration
Route 67
Johnstown, NY 12095

Genesee Community College
Hospitality Management
One College Road
Batavia, NY 14020

Herkimer County Community College
Food Service Administration
Reservoir Road
Herkimer, NY 13357

Hudson Valley Community College
Food Service Administration Department
80 Vandenburgh Avenue
Troy, NY 12180

Jefferson Community College
Hospitality and Tourism

Outer Coffeen Street
Watertown, NY 13601

Fiorello H. LaGuardia Community College
Dietetic Technician Program
31–10 Thomson Avenue
Long Island City, NY 11101

Mohawk Valley Community College
Food Service
Floyd Avenue
Rome, NY 13440

Monroe Community College
Food Service Administration
100 East Henrietta Road
Rochester, NY 14623

Nassau Community College
Hotel/Restaurant Technology
Stewart Avenue
Garden City, NY 11530

New York City Technical College
Hotel and Restaurant Management Department
300 Jay Street
Brooklyn, NY 11201

New York Institute of Dietetics
Food and Hotel Management
154 West 14th Street
New York, NY 10011

New York University
Foodservice Management Program
239 Greene Street, 537 East Building
New York, NY 10003

The New York Restaurant School
The New School for Social Research
27 West 34th Street
New York, NY 10001

Niagara County Community College
Food Service/Professional Chef Option
3111 Saunders Settlement Road
Sanborn, NY 14132

Onondaga Community College
Foodservice Administration and Hotel Management
Route #173
Syracuse, NY 13215

Schenectady County Community College
Hotel Technology and Culinary Arts
Washington Avenue
Schenectady, NY 12305

Paul Smith's College of Arts & Sciences
Hotel/Restaurant Management and Chef Training
Paul Smiths, NY 12970

State University of New York at Alfred
Food Service
South Brooklyn Avenue
Wellsville, NY 14895

State University of New York at Canton
Hotel Technology, Restaurant Management
Cornell Drive
Canton, NY 13617

State University of New York at Cobleskill
Food Service and Hospitality Administration
Champlin Hall
Cobleskill, NY 12043

State University of New York at Delhi
Hotel, Restaurant and Food Service Management
Delhi, NY 13753

State University of New York at Farmingdale
Food Service Administration/Restaurant Management
Melville Road
Farmingdale, NY 11735

State University of New York at Morrisville
Food Science Technology
Bailey Annex
Morrisville, NY 13408

Suffolk County Community College
Dietetic Technician
Speonk Riverhead Road
Riverhead, NY 11901

Sullivan County Community College
Hotel Technology
Loch Sheldrake, NY 12759

Tompkins Cortland Community College
Hotel Technology/Food Service Administration
170 North Street
Dryden, NY 13053

Villa Maria College of Buffalo
Food Service Management
240 Pine Ridge Road
Buffalo, NY 14225

Westchester Community College
Hotel and Restaurant Management
75 Grasslands Road
Valhalla, NY 10595

NORTH CAROLINA

Asheville Buncombe Technical College
Culinary Technology and Motel and Restaurant Management
340 Victoria Road
Asheville, NC 28801

Central Piedmont Community College
Hotel, Restaurant Management Program
P.O. Box 35009
Charlotte, NC 28235

Fayetteville Technical Institute
Food Service Management
P.O. Box 35236
Fayetteville, NC 28303

Lenoir Community College
Food Service Management
P.O. Box 188
Kinston, NC 28502

Southwestern Technical College
Food Service Management
P.O. Box 67
Sylva, NC 28779

Wilkes Community College
Hotel/Restaurant Management
Drawer 120
Wilkesboro, NC 28697

NORTH DAKOTA

Bismarck Junior College
Hotel, Motel and Restaurant Management
Shafer Heights
Bismarck, ND 58501

North Dakota State School of Science
Cook and Chef Training
Wahpeton, ND 58075

OHIO

Bowling Green State University
Applied Sciences Department
901 Rye Beach Road
Huron, OH 44839

Cincinnati Technical College
Executive Chef Technology/Hotel-Motel-Restaurant Management
3520 Central Parkway
Cincinnati, OH 45223

Clermont General and Technical College
University of Cincinnati
Hospitality Management
College Drive
Batavia, OH 45103

Columbus Technical Institute
Hospitality Management Department
550 East Spring Street
Columbus, OH 43215

Cuyahoga Community College
Hospitality Management
2900 Community College Road
Cleveland, OH 44115

Hocking Technical College
Hotel/Restaurant Management
Route #1
Nelsonville, OH 45764

Jefferson Technical College
Hospitality/Food Service Management
4000 Sunset Boulevard
Steubenville, OH 43952

Owens Technical College
Hospitality Management Technology
30335 Oregon Road
Toledo, OH 43699

Terra Technical College
Hospitality Management
1220 Cedar Street
Fremont, OH 43420

University of Toledo—Community and Technical College
Food Service Management/Culinary Arts
West Bancroft Street
Toledo, OH 43606

Youngstown State University
Food and Nutrition/Dietetics
410 Wick Avenue
Youngstown, OH 44555

OKLAHOMA

Carl Albert Junior College
School of Hotel and Restaurant Management
P.O. Box 606
Poteau, OK 74953

Great Plains Area Vocational Technical Center
Commercial Food Services/Fast Foods Management
4500 West Lee Boulevard
Lawton, OK 73505

Indian Meridian Vocational Technical School
Commercial Food Production and Management
1312 South Sangre Road
Stillwater, OK 74074

Oklahoma State University School of Technical Training
Food Service
4th and Mission
Okmulgee, OK 74447

Pioneer Area Vocational Technical School
Commercial Foods
2101 North Ash
Ponca City, OK 74601

Southern Oklahoma Area Vocational-Technical School
Culinary Arts
Route 1
Ardmore, OK 73401

Tulsa Junior College
Lodging and Food Service Management
909 South Boston
Tulsa, OK 74119

OREGON

Chemeketa Community College
Food Service Management

P.O. Box 14007
Salem, OR 97309

Lane Community College
Food Service Management
4000 East 30th Avenue
Eugene, OR 97405

Linn-Benton Community College
Culinary Arts/Restaurant Management
6500 SW Pacific Boulevard
Albany, OR 97321

Portland Community College
Hotel/Motel or Restaurant Management/Sous Chef
12000 SW 49th
Portland, OR 97219

PENNSYLVANIA

Community College of Allegheny County
Hospitality Management/Culinary Arts
595 Beatty Road
Monroeville, PA 15146

Bucks County Community College
Hotel, Motel and Institutional Management/Culinary Arts
Swamp Road
Newtown, PA 18940

Butler County Community College
Food Service Management
Oak Hills, College Drive
Butler, PA 16001

Delaware County Community College
Hotel/Restaurant Management
Route 252
Media, PA 19063

Harrisburg Area Community College
Food Service Management
3300 Cameron Street
Harrisburg, PA 17110

Keystone Junior College
Hospitality Management
La Plume, PA 18440

Luzerne County Community College
Hotel and Restaurant Management
Prospect Street and Middle Road
Nanticoke, PA 18643

Montgomery County Community College
Hospitality Management Program
340 DeKalb Pike
Blue Bell, PA 19422

Peirce Junior College
Hospitality Management
1420 Pine Street
Philadelphia, PA 19102

Pennsylvania State University, Berks Campus
Hotel and Food Service
College of Human Development
R.D. #5, Tulpehocken Road
Reading, PA 19608

Community College of Philadelphia
Hotel, Restaurant and Institutional Management
1700 Spring Garden Street
Philadelphia, PA 19130

The Restaurant School
Restaurant Management/Chef Training
2129 Walnut Street
Philadelphia, PA 19103

Westmoreland County Community College
Food Service Management/Culinary Arts
Armbrust Road
Youngwood, PA 15697

Williamsport Area Community College
Food and Hospitality Management
1005 West Third Street
Williamsport, PA 17701

RHODE ISLAND

Johnson and Wales College
Hotel Management/Culinary Arts
8 Abbott Park Place
Providence, RI 02903

SOUTH CAROLINA

Greenville Technical College
Food Science
P.O. Box 5616—Station "B"
Greenville, SC 29606

Horry-Georgetown Technical College
Hotel, Motel and Restaurant Management

Highway 501 East, P.O. Box 1966
Conway, SC 29526

University of South Carolina
Hotel, Restaurant and Tourism Administration
084 Coliseum—District A-1
Columbia, SC 29208

SOUTH DAKOTA

Black Hills State College
Travel Industry Management
1200 University
Spearfish, SD 57783

Mitchell Area Vocational Technical School
Cook/Chef
821 North Capitol
Mitchell, SD 57301

TENNESSEE

Knoxville State Area Vocational Technical School
Commercial Food Preparation
1100 Liberty Street
Knoxville, TN 37919

Nashville Area Vocational Technical School
Commercial Foods
2601 Bransford Avenue
Nashville, TN 37207

Shelby State Community College
Department of Nutrition and Dietetics
P.O. Box 40568
Memphis, TN 38104

State Technical Institute at Memphis
Motel/Restaurant Management Technology
5983 Macon Cove
Memphis, TN 38184

TEXAS

Central Texas College
Food Service and Hotel/Motel Management
Highway 190 West
Killeen, TX 76542

Del Mar College
Restaurant Management Department

Baldwin at Ayers
Corpus Christi, TX 78404

El Centro College
Food Service Operations
Main at Lamar Streets
Dallas, TX 75202

Hill Junior College
Food Preparation, Service and Management
Box 619
Hillsboro, TX 76645

Houston Community College
Culinary Arts
1300 Holman
Houston, TX 77004

Houston Community College
Hotel, Restaurant, Club Management
4310 Dunlavy
Houston, TX 77006

Northwood Institute—Texas
Hotel/Restaurant Management
P.O. Box 58 FR 1382
Cedar Hill, TX 75401

St. Philip's College
Hospitality Management/Chefs Apprenticeship
2111 Nevada
San Antonio, TX 78203

San Jacinto College
Restaurant Management and Dietetic Technology
8060 Spencer Highway
Pasadena, TX 77505

San Jacinto College—North Campus
Baking and Catering
5800 Uvalde
Houston, TX 77049

South Plains College—Lubbock
Food Industry Management
1302 Main Street
Lubbock, TX 79401

Texas State Technical Institute
Food Service Technology Program
Building 15–1
Waco, TX 76705

UTAH
Utah Technical College
Hotel-Motel/Restaurant Management
P.O. Box 1609
Provo UT 84601

VERMONT
Ethan Allen Community College
Hotel/Restaurant Management
310 Bonnet Street
Manchester Center, VT 05255

Champlain College
Hotel, Motel and Restaurant Management
232 South Willard Street
Burlington, VT 05402

New England Culinary Institute
Culinary Arts
110 East State Street
Montpelier, VT 05602

VIRGINIA
Thomas Nelson Community College
Hotel, Restaurant and Institutional Management
P.O. Box 9407
Hampton, VA 23670

Northern Virginia Community College
Hotel, Restaurant and Institutional Management
8333 Little River Turnpike
Annandale, VA 22003

Tidewater Community College
Hotel, Restaurant and Institutional Management
1700 College Crescent
Virginia Beach, VA 23456

John Tyler Community College
Food Service Management
Chester, VA 23831

WASHINGTON
Clark College
Culinary Arts

1800 East McLoughlin Boulevard
Vancouver, WA 98663

Everett Community College
Food Technology
801 Wetmore Avenue
Everett, WA 98201

Fort Steilacoom Community College
Food Service Management
P.O. Box 33265
Fort Lewis, WA 98433

Highline Community College
Hospitality and Tourism Management
Pacific Highway South and South 240th
Midway, WA 98032

North Seattle Community College
Restaurant Management/Culinary Arts
9600 College Way North
Seattle, WA 98103

Olympic College
Commercial Cooking/Food Service
16th and Chester
Bremerton, WA 98310

Seattle Central Community College
Hospitality Management/Culinary Arts
1702 Harvard Avenue
Seattle, WA 98122

Shoreline Community College
Food Services Technology
16101 Greenwood Avenue North
Seattle, WA 98133

Skagit Valley College
Culinary Arts/Restaurant Management
2405 College Way
Mount Vernon, WA 98273

South Seattle Community College
Food Service Management/Pastry and Specialty Baking
6000 16th Avenue SW
Seattle, WA 98106

Spokane Community College
Culinary Arts/Hotel-Motel Management
1810 North Green Street
Spokane, WA 99207

WEST VIRGINIA

Fairmont State College
Food Service Management
Home Economics/Technology
Fairmont, WV 26554

Garnet Career Center
Commercial Foods
422 Dickinson Street
Charleston WV 25301

James Rumsey Vocational Technical Center
Food Service Occupations
Route 6—Box 268
Martinsburg, WV 25401

Shepherd College
Hotel, Motel and Restaurant Management
Shepherdstown, WV 25443

West Virginia State College
Hotel, Restaurant and Institutional Management
Campus Box 53
Institute, WV 25112

WISCONSIN

District 1 Technical Insitute
Restaurant and Hotel Cookery; Hospitality Management
620 West Clairemont Avenue
Eau Claire, WI 54701

Fox Valley Technical Institute
Home and Consumer Sciences Division
1825 North Bluemound Drive
Appleton, WI 54913

Gateway Technical Institute
Hotel/Motel Management; Food Service Management
1001 South Main Street
Racine, WI 53403

Madison Area Technical College
Industrial Foods
211 North Carroll Street
Madison, WI 53703

Milwaukee Area Technical College
Restaurant and Hotel Cookery Program
1015 North Sixth Street
Milwaukee, WI 53203

Moraine Park Technical Institute
Restaurant and Hotel Cookery
235 North National Avenue
Fond du Lac, WI 54935

Nicolet College
Hospitality Management
Box 518
Rhinelander, WI 54501

Southwest Wisconsin Vocational Technical Institute
Food Service Management
Route #1, Box 500
Fennimore, WI 53809

Western Wisconsin Technical Institute
Food Service Management
Eighth and Pine Streets
La Crosse, WI 54601

Wisconsin Indianhead Technical Institute
Hospitality Management—Tourism
2100 Beaser Avenue
Ashland, WI 54806

WYOMING

Laramie County Community College
Food Services
1400 East College Drive
Cheyenne, WY 82007

Appendix **B**

Sources of Further Information

American Culinary Federation
P.O. Box 3466
St. Augustine, FL 32084

Council on Hotel, Restaurant and Institutional Education
1522 K Street NW
Washington, DC 20007

Educational Institute of the American Hotel and
Motel Association
1407 South Harrison Road
East Lansing, MI 48823

International Association of Cooking Professionals
1001 Connecticut Avenue, NW
Washington, DC 20036

National Association of Trade and Technical Schools
2251 Wisconsin Avenue NW
Washington, DC 20007

National Institute for the Foodservice Industry
20 North Wacker Drive
Chicago, IL 60606

National Restaurant Association
One Park Place
Chicago, IL 60601

School of Hotel, Restaurant and Institutional Management
Michigan State University
East Lansing, MI 48223

Appendix C

Reading List

Capone, Carol Ann. *Opportunities in Food Services.* Lincolnwood, IL: VGM Career Horizons Book, 1984.

Cavallara, Ann. *Careers in Food Services.* New York: Elseview/ Nelson Books, 1981.

de Voss, Lishka. *How to Be a Professional Waiter or Waitress.* New York: St. Martins Press, 1985.

Dyer, Dewey. *So You Want to Start a Restaurant.* New York: Van Nostrand Reinhold Co., 1981.

Franchise Opportunities Handbook. Andrew Kosteuka, comp. Washington, DC: United States Department of Commerce, 1985.

Herbert, Jack. *Creating a Successful Restaurant.* New York: St. Martins Press, 1985.

Kahrl, William. *Planning and Operating a Successful Food Service Operation.* New York: Lebnar-Friedman, Inc., 1979.

Luxemberg, Stan. *Road Side Empires: How the Chains Franchised America.* New York: Viking, 1985.

Miller, Daniel. *Starting a Small Restaurant.* Boston: Harvard Common Press, 1978.

Peck, Ralph. *Hotel and Motel Careers.* New York: Franklin Watts, 1977.

Ray, Mary Frey. *Exploring Professional Cooking.* Peoria, IL: Charles Bennett Co., 1980.

Robbins, Charles. *So You Want to Open a Restaurant.* San Francisco: Harbor Publishing, 1982.

Shown, Janet. *Free Lance Food Crafting: How to Become Profitably Self-Employed in Your Own Creative Cooking*

Business. Boulder, CO: Live Oak Publications, 1983. (This book describes how to start a cooking school, run a gourmet shop, and start a take-out shop.)

Stokes, John. *How to Manage a Restaurant or Institutional Food Service*. Dubuque, IA: Wm.C. Brown Co., 1981.

Taylor, Derek. *How to Sell Banquets*. Boston: CBI Publishing Co., 1981.

Two more advanced, technical books for foodservice professionals can be purchased from CBI Book Department, ACT Company, P.O. Box 429474, Cincinnati, OH 45242. They are:

The Culinary Institute of America. *The Professional Chef*, 4th ed., 1986.

Peddersen, Raymond. *Foodservice and Hotel Purchasing*.

Index